You Are He

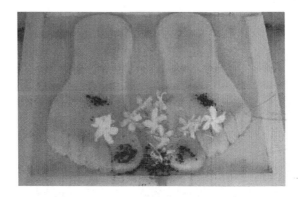

Commentaries On the Teaching
of Sri Ranjit Maharaj

Andrew Vernon

Golden Day

ISBN: 978-0-6151-5603-3

Copyright © 2003 by Andrew Vernon
www.wayofthebird.com

Preface: How to Use This Book

Sri Ranjit Maharaj called the way of understanding, or Self-enquiry, the bird's way, in contrast to meditation, which he called the ant's way. The ant goes very slowly and, if it tries to climb a forest tree, it may die before it reaches the destination. The bird, on the other hand, flies easily from branch to branch. Maharaj always taught that you are yourself the reality, and so you are already free, free as a bird, without limits. You are He, the reality, right now, only you do not know it with certainty. To have that understanding of who you are, you must get rid of the false notion that you are something other than that reality.

Meditation, chanting a mantra, and various kinds of physical and mental disciplines may be useful to prepare the mind for understanding, but the end of seeking is not reached until there is Self-knowledge. The solution has to involve Self-knowledge because the problem is one of Self-ignorance. No spiritual practices that you undertake can solve that problem. You can meditate six hours at a stretch and enjoy blissful states, but as soon as you stop that activity, you are back in ignorance again! You have to find the answer to the question "Who am I?" When you know that, ignorance disappears and you know everything that you need to know.

That is what the Way of the Bird is all about. It means taking the time to think deeply about the teaching, not accepting it blindly, but experiencing everything and verifying everything for yourself.

I wrote these commentaries on Maharaj's teaching because some people have said that they find his ideas difficult to understand and would like additional explanation. The commentaries attempt to provide this explanation, or at least offer some ways to think about the concepts involved.

Maharaj taught in a traditional lineage of Masters in Maharashtra, in central India. His style of teaching was to take a question and then answer it by talking for half an hour or forty-five minutes. When he spoke, he rarely stopped to expand on the individual ideas he expressed, but preferred to layer one powerful and profound concept on another in a continuous flow. Personally, I always found it very useful, for the purposes of study, to consider his ideas one by one, as aphorisms or *sutras*. Taken in this way, the individual ideas can be easier to approach and easier to understand. You will find 366 of these ideas in this book, and together they cover all the essential concepts of *Advaita Vedanta*, as well as presenting a practical method of working with them.

If you look at the Table of Contents that follows this preface, you will notice a few things (apart from the fact that it is unusually long!):

- It has a chapter for each month.
- Each chapter consists of numbered sections, one for each day of that month.
- Each section heading is actually a quotation.

If you wish to contemplate one of these quotations every day of the year, you can easily do so by looking up the numbered quotation for that day. The commentaries elaborate the quotations, but you may prefer simply to reflect on the quotations by themselves. In that case, you will find that the essence of this teaching is in the Table of Contents. On the other hand, you don't need to associate the quotes with particular days. If you prefer to just read the book from front to back, you can do that as well. The book includes a glossary that explains the terms that Maharaj used.

Andrew Vernon, Marin County, California, October 2003.

Contents

1

January: The Illusory Nature of the World

1.1 "The world is not true."

The world is not external. Perception of the world happens spontaneously in the Self, against the unchanging background of reality, like the dream that occurs in sleep. You are that Self, not an individual, but you have forgotten about it. In fact, the individual person that appears to have forgotten is also happening spontaneously as one of the characters in the dream of life, while the Self rests peacefully in its own completeness, like *Vishnu* sleeping on the cosmic ocean. If a world appears, there is consciousness of it; if nothing appears, there is no consciousness of it. The world that appears could be a dream world or it could be this waking world. The appearance and the one who perceives it arise together and are not separate. Both the dream world and the waking world disappear when you are deeply asleep. If they were true, they would remain.

1.2 "The body is dead at this moment."

The body is like an appliance that works when electricity is connected to it and which ceases to function when the power is disconnected. The body itself, like the appliance, is an inert thing—it doesn't have any life of its own. The life that animates the body is a power that transcends the sense of individual existence. What is the nature of that power that gives life to all that lives? That power is pure knowledge or universal consciousness. As long as that power is connected, what we call life is there. It is there even when the body and mind subside into the state called deep sleep (dreamless sleep), which is proven by the fact that when you wake up in the morning, you say "I slept well." Such knowledge would be impossible if power had not been continuous during the sleeping state.

The power prompts two living cells: male and female, to unite and form the gross physical body in the first place, and continues to make it grow to maturity. It remains for the span of time allotted to the body, and in the end drops the body. Where does the power go? It doesn't go anywhere, because it is all-pervasive. The body disintegrates, returning to the gross elements from which it was formed.

1.3 "Be always courageous. Say that nothing is true."

If you say "nothing is true," that is an act of courage because you have to make that statement without any support from the world. If you read the newspaper, ask your relatives, or look anywhere outside, you will not find any evidence to support it. Worst of all, there is no support from your own perceptions either—your own eyes see the world as a collection of separate objects and your mind generally takes it to be true. Yet Maharaj said that one who takes the world to be true remains an aspirant, while one who does not take it to be true becomes a realized person! This is why faith is so important.

Only faith in the Master allows you to keep returning to the thought that his point of view is correct. You have to rely on faith until you realize the truth of what he says for yourself. As an aspirant, faith in the Master is really the most powerful weapon that you have. It is not different from grace. It can break down all the barriers that illusion places in the way of your aspiration and can dissolve the veil of ignorance. Where there is faith, the power to accept and understand the Master's teaching is there as well.

1.4 "The world is only thought."

Imagine what would happen if you suddenly found yourself without thought and without the possibility of thought. How would the world appear to you then? Would you see any world of separate objects? Could you recognize this room, this page, these words? Could you experience emotions?

You would not recognize any separate objects, and you would not see anything apart from yourself. Your own awareness would constitute the whole of reality. The so-called objective world; that is, the world that is apparently full of separate objects, is really an illusion. It exists only as names and forms. The mind is not the cause of that world-projection; it is only the mechanism through which the divine power (pure knowledge or universal consciousness) is working. That consciousness is all-pervasive and so it is the underlying reality of the apparent objects, including the apparent person who perceives them.

1.5 "Have fear of nothing and no one, for everything is nothing."

In the vision of a realized person, there is nothing apart from the Self. Compared to that reality, everything that appears is nothing but a passing show. Absence of fear comes from the knowledge that what you are will not perish. This is why Maharaj gave the example that if someone comes and holds a revolver to your head, you should be able to say "That's OK. It's only the name and form that dies. I don't die." This may seem extreme, but is a statement that indicates what the goal is. As long as you are an aspirant, of course, it would be natural for fear to arise in that situation, because the certainty that you are not the body is not there. Certainty means that you know the answer to the question "Who am I?" beyond any doubt. Fear of death is therefore a clear indication that you still have to find the answer to that question.

1.6 "All the ornaments are nothing but gold."

In India, when gold ornaments are sold, the value is calculated according to the weight of the gold. For example, five bangles are 100 grams of gold, and a necklace is 100 grams of gold as well. The form can be one thing or another thing; the underlying substance is what matters. This analogy means that all the various forms in the world are nothing but *Brahman*, the all-pervading consciousness. There is really nothing that separates one ornament from another as long as you are looking just at the gold. In the same way, there is nothing to distinguish one form from another if it is understood that there is one reality underlying them all.

1.7 "The body is only a covering on me."

In Vedanta, the body is actually only one of five coverings, or *kosas*. All these coverings, from the most subtle to the most gross (which is the body) are only an appearance on the screen of reality. If you take the body to be something that has some independent existence, you are making a mistake. (Saint Tukaram said "I committed a criminal mistake, taking the body as true.") The body is an illusion. It comes, stays for a while, and then goes. Problems arise only when you take yourself to be that illusion. If you see the illusion as illusion, there is no problem; it can remain there without doing any harm.

1.8 "When the breath goes, nothing remains."

Knowledge of your existence as a living being depends upon the presence of the gross physical body. The food eaten by the body is processed and the most refined product of that process is the knowledge "I am." That knowledge is what allows you to experience everything in this world and to act in it. According to *Vedanta*, the number of breaths that the body will take is predetermined and, when that number is reached, the body falls away. At that point, there will indeed be nothing remaining, because knowledge depends on the body, and the whole appearance of the world depends on knowledge. If you have identified yourself with that concept of "I," then you will fear death, because death is the end of that "I." With Self-knowledge, however, you understand that your true being is beyond knowledge. You also know that it will not be affected by the disappearance of the "I" concept, anymore than it was affected by its appearance.

1.9 "Say what is true is true, what is not true is not true always."

One way of looking at the fundamental problem of living is to see that you feel a lack of completeness, of wholeness. You then try to find the solution to the problem by seeking happiness in external things. This error is based on the unquestioned assumption that the world is true. Maharaj therefore urged his disciples to constantly question this assumption and to go against it by asserting its opposite. The purpose of this assertion is to establish a habit of correct thinking to replace the old, wrong thinking. There are of course limitations to this approach. The fundamental problem is a problem of Self-ignorance, and it can only be resolved by Self-knowledge. Right thinking, in the sense of repetition of the correct ideas, is not an end in itself, but only one of the means, another way to make the mind subtle and to prepare it for the understanding of 'Who am I.'

1.10 "Everything is nothing."

What kind of logic makes "everything" equal to "nothing?" "Everything" here means every object that can be perceived, including thoughts and feelings as well as gross objects. All of it taken together is referred to in the Upanishads as "this" (*idam*), as opposed to reality, which is referred to as "that" (*tat*). "Nothing" means not having independent existence. Note that "nothing" does not mean "having no existence of any kind." It means that the existence that objects have is only apparent (*mithya* in traditional Vedanta teaching). The appearance depends on the underlying reality, just as the waves depend on the underlying ocean. The waves do not exist by themselves. They exist in one sense, because there is the concept-word "waves" that we use to label them, just as we also label the "ocean" that the waves are part of. However, neither waves nor ocean are really anything but water.

1.11 "Nothing happens and nothing is true."

Think about the events that happened to you ten years ago. What remains of all that occurred, all the suffering and heartbreak, all the joy and affection? Where has it all gone? It has disappeared just as though it had never existed. The same thing is happening to your experience today. This very moment has arrived, bringing with it its particular experience, only to disappear almost instantly. When death comes to the body, what will the whole life have amounted to? What will be the sum total of reality that has been accumulated through these passing experiences? The answer is zero. Nothing happens and nothing has ever happened. It was all a dream. Only the unchanging background, against which all these experiences appear and fade, is real. Shakespeare wrote in *The Tempest*:

And, like the baseless fabric of this vision,
The cloud-capp'd towers, the gorgeous palaces,
Yea, all which it inherit, shall dissolve
And, like this insubstantial pageant faded,
Leave not a rack behind.

1.12 "Be indifferent to things because they don't exist."

Suppose you were to wake up in the middle of a dream and find yourself moving and acting in it. You see all the scenery and all the people, including yourself. However, at the same time, you remain aware of yourself as the one in whom the dream is taking place. Wouldn't you then be totally indifferent to the objects and the circumstances of the dream? This is the kind of indifference that the realized person has.

Detachment from the objects of the world happens naturally, without any effort, simply because they are seen to be nothing.

1.13 "If you say "It's all wrong," you're a king. If you say "It's true," you're a slave."

Things are not what they seem. The prevalent notion that one is a person living one's own life is an illusion. Actually, all that exists is totally free consciousness that is not involved in the self-regulating show of the world. The one who knows this and sees this is the king, the one who is above the law. The ignorant person who takes the show to be real remains in slavery to the body and mind.

1.14 "Nothing is bad, nothing is good, because it is not."

Maharaj frequently said that there is no bad and no good in the world. By this, he meant to remind us of how things are in reality. If something is not true, what meaning is there in saying it is good or bad? The distinction is only valid for one who identifies with the form of world, taking it to be true. Concepts of good and bad are nothing but imagination and apply to nothing but illusion. In the purity and sacredness of the Self there is no duality. In fact there is no concept at all in that Oneness.

1.15 "Mind always takes you out of the reality."

If you were a wave on the ocean and you started thinking of yourself as a separate individual, you would live on the surface and be whipped about this way and that, and you would lose touch with your reality, which is the water that you are made from. This is what happens to the ignorant mind. It is not separate from *Brahman*, the universal consciousness, but it has picked up the idea that it is separate. As long as this illusion persists, the mind will continue to appear to take you out of the reality.

1.16 "The world you see is nothing but a reflection of reality. Reflection cannot be true."

Here Maharaj offers another way to approach the idea that the world is not true. Reality is absolute awareness, but it cannot perceive itself because it is One. In order for the absolute knowledge even to know that it exists, it must manifest itself and become two. The world is the mirror that the Absolute holds up in order to see Itself. The reflection has no existence in itself. This act of manifestation is the creation of duality, and in duality, the whole world appears. In the first chapter of the *Amritanubhav*, Jnaneshwar, the great Maratha saint of the twelfth century, describes this appearance of the world as the play of *Shiva* (the unmanifest Absolute) and *Shakti* (the manifest divine power):

Through Her,
The absolute void becomes the manifest world;
But Her existence is derived from Her Lord.
Shiva himself became His beloved;
But without Her presence,
No universe exists.

1.17 "When you say that the reflection is true, you are lost."

It would certainly be very strange if, when one saw one's face in a mirror, one were to suppose that there was a person there. It is perfectly obvious that one is the cause of that reflection. Yet this does not happen with the world in general. The mind is turned outward and takes the reflection to be real and forgets that all appearance depends entirely on the existence of the one who perceives it. The root cause of the illusion of the world is forgetting your true Self. You remember yourself and think of yourself as the body, the mind, and the ego. However, to remember yourself as the ego is to forget that you are the Self, the reality. When you forget that you are the Self, you are lost because you do not realize that the reflections are not separate from the Self. They appear to have an existence or a life of their own.

1.18 "As long as duality is there, no happiness is possible."

Duality appears together with the sense of individual existence. It's a package deal. As soon as you subscribe to "I am this," you automatically get "I am not that" as well. When duality operates in this way, the sense of separation from everything else, that is everything that is perceived as "not-I," is inevitable. Actually, you even conceive of the Self, which you always are, to be something separate from you. You then think of it as an object to be attained and start to search for yourself! What could be more ludicrous? In duality, everything becomes wrong. It goes without saying that happiness, other than the most fleeting taste, is not possible in these mixed-up circumstances.

1.19 "The wheel of suffering happens because you say it's mine."

The concept of "mine" only makes sense in the context of duality and separation. In Oneness, there is nothing that is mine, just as there is nothing that is not mine. The suffering of separation from the world and from oneself, happens because you accept the concept of "I." Because you have taken delivery of that concept (as Sri Nisargadatta Maharaj said), you also have to take delivery of all the other concepts that come with it: "I suffer," "I am lacking something," "I need to take care of what is mine," and so on. The wheel of suffering continues to turn until the I-concept is rejected as false.

1.20 "Duality makes you."

The very nature of the illusory life as an individual human being is duality. The whole world appearance is based on the notion that "I" am here and there is the world out there. This division is a concept and has no basis in reality, which is One. Where does the notion of duality come from? It is built into consciousness itself. Every living being is a form of consciousness and has the sense of "I am," in humans as a thought, and in other sentient beings as the sense of individual existence. That is the nature of manifest consciousness. You cannot avoid duality, because to be conscious of yourself as "I" means that you have to be conscious of the "not-I" that is everything else. This condition is transcended by the understanding that "I" does not refer to the separate individual but to the non-dual reality that underlies it.

1.21 "Anything you see is not there. It is space, it is zero."

Twentieth century atomic physics demonstrated that all matter is nothing but energy. This evidence appeared a few thousand years after the sages of ancient India expressed the same truth in the Upanishads! The physical eyes of the human body of course cannot see objects as space or energy. Because of the limitations of visual perception, we see objects as colored forms with edges that appear to separate them from other forms. This is no more a "correct" way of seeing solid, three-dimensional objects than if one was to see them as luminous, amorphous, animated beings. However, it is what we are accustomed to.

Vedanta states that the objects of the world are "*namarupa*" only. *Nama* means name and *rupa* means form. The forms and their names go together in the mental process of perception and recognition. Both are projections on the non-dual reality, in the same way that images are projected on a screen. The images are only colored light, the light itself is uncolored. Objects, although they appear to have form, and are recognized by their names, are still non-separate from the space that pervades them. Space allows all the forms of the world to appear. But reality is subtler than space, because it is aware of it.

1.22 "Truth always remains the truth. What is not true never existed."

What does it mean that something is true? It means that it exists, it is real. Truth is not an idea or a set of ideas but is a word-pointer to that which never comes and never goes away, that which can always be relied upon. The words reality, truth, existence are all pointers to that which always remains. Truth has permanent being, or existence. That which is not true, on the other hand, does not have any reality and cannot exist, has never existed.

1.23 "All is illusion, but to understand the illusion, illusion is needed."

Meeting the Master and accepting the Master's teaching occurs in illusion; like an encounter in a dream. However, to understand that illusion is illusion, it is necessary to go through the phase of acquiring knowledge and applying it to oneself. The knowledge that the Master provides in the form of teaching is ultimately not true, in the sense that the teaching is essentially just a system of ideas or set of concepts offered to the aspirant as a way to make sense of his or her experiences. Ideas and concepts, however useful within the illusion, are still within that illusion and so are not true.

Acceptance of the Master's teaching happens because of the faith that the aspirant has in the Master, even though that separation between Master and aspirant is also ultimately false. Despite it all, understanding and self-realization do occur for the aspirant. Once that realization has occurred, the Master's teachings are no longer needed, just as when you reach the shore, you leave the boat at the water's edge.

1.24 "If it is not true, just let it be. Why to harm or demolish what is not?"

Generally speaking, it is not necessary to do anything about the external circumstances of one's life. When you are an aspirant, you need to make sure that you have the qualifications needed to receive and accept knowledge from the Master. Apart from that, you can simply let life continue, while focusing free time and energy on understanding the teaching. Trying to demolish the ego or force the mind to stop its flow of thoughts is counter-productive. Such "efforts" only strengthen the sense of doership of the ego. After realization, it is very clear that there is nothing that needs to be done because there is no false concept of a "doer." Life with its ever changing patterns goes on, but the realized person remains one with the unchanging reality that is always there in the background.

1.25 "What is there when everything is zero? What is true?"

Maharaj would often say "Nothing is true." Someone would ask "Surely your words are true?" But he would reply "No, Master's words are not true and Master is not true either." So when he said "nothing" he really meant it! One way to look at this is to break up the word "nothing" into "no thing," so that the phrase becomes "no thing is true."

Imagine a balance with Zero on one side and One on the other. Anything that can be objectified—thoughts, feelings, sensations, and experiences, as well as what we consider to be physical objects in the gross world—all this is placed on the zero side of the balance and is called "this," (*idam* in Sanskrit). On the other side of the balance—the One side—is that which can never be objectified, but which is always there. It is not a "thing" and is called "that" (*tat* in Sanskrit). That is what is true.

1.26 "All is wrong, nothing is true. Everyone is running in the wrong direction."

Maharaj sometimes quoted a sentence that his Master, Sri Siddharameshwar Maharaj, wrote in a small book called *The Golden Day*: "The whole world is galloping toward Hell." In that book, Siddharameshwar Maharaj comments on how all the inventions and devices of the twentieth century only increased the stress and unhappiness in peoples' lives. More and more emphasis was being placed on seeking satisfaction in the pursuit of a fast-paced, pleasure-oriented lifestyle. He wrote his critique in India in the 1930s. What would he have said if he had lived to see the 1990s? The power of the so-called "wisdom of the world" traps almost everybody. In Vedanta, it is said that millions of lives may pass before there is a human birth in which there is a longing for God and all the necessary qualifications to seek Him. Only when that longing is there will someone start running in the right direction.

1.27 "What you know is nothing. If it is true, you cannot know it."

It is characteristic of the ego that it believes that it knows everything it needs to know. Many people speak and act as though they know exactly what the world is like, the right way to live, the correct way to behave. They never question the validity of their opinions. Scientists, materials, atheists, as well as believers in one or the other of the established religions, all feel that they have the inside track to the truth. And yet all of this scientific and worldly knowledge is knowledge of nothing. Knowledge of objects does not last. It disappears altogether when the knower goes to sleep. That which truly exists, the Self, cannot be known because it is not an object. Can the eyes see themselves? Can the tongue taste itself? Can the knower know itself? The Self is what you are. You cannot get outside of it in order to know it.

1.28 "The illusion cannot give something more to reality, because reality is at the base of everything that is."

All the fascinating places and magnificent scenery in the world, all the beautiful plants and flowers, the enormous variety of species of animals and the multitudes of human beings—none of them have any effect on the Self. They do not add anything to reality when they appear and they do not take anything away from reality when they go away. Reality, the Self, is the base of all that appears, the source. It remains full and complete in Itself if there are a billion worlds, and it remains full and complete if there is no manifestation at all. The Sanskrit prayer at the beginning of the *Isha Upanishad* expresses this great truth:

Om purnamadah, purnamidam purnat purnamudacyate
Punasya purnamadaya purnamevavasisyate

This is complete, that is complete;
From completeness completeness came forth;
Taking completeness from completeness;
Adding completeness to completeness,
Completeness alone remains.

1.29 "When nothing is, all is only beliefs and concepts of the mind."

We live in an interpreted world. The world in itself has no meaning; it has only the meaning that we give to it. A small child does not experience a world of things, of separate objects, but experiences only itself. Gradually, as concepts and beliefs accumulate, the world takes shape together with, and based on, the "I" sense. Nothing (no thing) is outside of that sense of one's own existence. Everything (every thing) is contained within it. The multiplicity of the apparent creation emerges from the "I" sense like a great tree unfolding itself from a small seed. The appearance of the gross world depends on the thoughts and concepts of the subtle world, and the appearance of the subtle world depends in turn on the space and nothingness of the causal world. Before the beginning, there is nothing there, and then, in the beginning, is "the Word." That word is "I."

1.30 "The five elements that compose the body return to the five elements. The power returns to the power. Only the name and form which are illusion disappear."

When death occurs, the elements of the gross body go back to dust and ashes, while the pure consciousness withdraws unstained by the individual form with which it was identified. What we call death is limited to the name and form. How are name and form illusion? Because they appear and disappear. If time could be accelerated by millions of times, one would see a human being emerge from nothing, grow from infancy to childhood to adulthood to old age and return to nothing in a matter of seconds. Even the fame of a Shakespeare would disappear after a few minutes. Such an experience of time would be unpleasant, because our senses are accustomed to a process of growth and decay that plays itself out much slower. However, it is not a less "correct" a way of seeing the process of appearance and disappearance, only an unfamiliar one. Reality does not enter into this cycle; it remains as the changeless background against which the play of birth and death takes place.

1.31 "Even though everything seems to be, nothing is. It is exactly like a card trick."

Sri Nisargadatta Maharaj said that although the world can be said to appear, it cannot be said to Be. That which has being has real existence, while that which only appears is not true. The power of *Maya* makes this world appear and tricks us into taking it to be true by veiling the Self with ignorance. In ignorance, you forget your true nature as the Self and take yourself to be one separate entity among many others. As long as you remain ignorant of the Self, you cannot see through the trick of the apparent creation. Self-enquiry, leading to Self-knowledge, removes this ignorance and with it the illusion of existence as a separate entity.

2

February: The Nature of Reality

2.1 "Use the power to know that reality."

The power that is in each individual is what Sri Nisargadatta Maharaj called your "capital." That knowledge "I am" has appeared and is available for a limited time for investment. The best way to invest that capital is to use it to pursue the Master's teaching to the end; that is, until Self-knowledge brings the complete conviction that you are indeed the final reality, the Self.

2.2 "I have no limits."

If reality were limited by anything, it would no longer be One, and no longer be complete. That which limited it would have to be apart from it, which would not be possible, because that would make two. This is why the appearance of the world cannot be considered as separate from the Absolute, but only as a reflection of It. Limitations are imposed by the mind, on the mind. It is only in thought that you suffer limitations, such as the concept of being a separate individual. What you are in your true nature is limitless awareness, free of the three types of limitation: time, space, and object-hood.

2.3 "Be always free-minded. Don't worry about anything."

To be completely free from worry is really only possible for a realized person, and this is, in fact, one of the characteristics usually attributed to such a person. As with many of the direct instructions that Maharaj gave, this one is an indication of the direction to follow; of what you should aspire to. You should not beat yourself up if you cannot be worry-free right away. However, by worrying less and less over time, you gain dispassion (*vairagya*) and free the mind from worldly bindings. As you do so, you understand more and more of the knowledge that the Master has given.

2.4 "Everything is superimposed on my real nature."

The concept of superimposition is very important in *Advaita Vedanta*, as taught by Shankaracharya and his lineage since the seventh century. Superimposition is the concept that is used to explain how it is that the appearance of the world does not disturb the Oneness of the non-dual reality. The classic example is the snake that is superimposed on a rope when the rope is seen in semi-darkness. The snake appears real and has the ability to evoke real fear. However, when a light is shone upon it, the rope-snake disappears. Actually, of course, it was never there. The rope was the only reality. The imaginary snake "resolves" itself back into its underlying foundation—the rope, which was the only thing that was real. In the same way, all the apparent objects of the world are superimposed by the mind on the underlying reality.

2.5 "He pervades everywhere."

In the first chapter of the *Amritanubhav,* Jnaneshwar writes a poetic description of the way in which the final reality, or *Parabrahman*, here symbolized as the god Shiva, becomes manifest, but without disturbing its non-dual nature. The whole chapter is worth reading over and over because it succeeds in conveying something of the paradoxical nature of reality, which can be one and yet two at the same time. Here is a typical verse:

It is Shiva alone who lives in all forms;
He is both the male and the female.
It is because of the union of these two complements
That the whole universe exists.

This is the manner in which reality pervades everywhere. Just as the light of the sun shines everywhere without taking anything away from the sun, the power of pure knowledge animates all living things without diminishing its source.

2.6 "There is only oneness in the world, no duality at all."

Everything that one sees or perceives is an appearance in awareness, but it does not affect or diminish that awareness in any way. This is the beauty and the mystery of the manifest reality. That which is seen and the seer of it are not-two, they are One, just as the shadow does not exist apart from the object that casts it, or the rays of the sun are not separate from the sun itself.

The Self is the only reality, the only One. That Self is the source of everything that appears. The world is not apart from the Self, but the Self is not contained by the world. It remains untouched just as the mirror is not altered by the reflection that appears in it.

Here are two more verses from the first chapter of the *Amritanubhav:*

The sun appears to shine because of its rays,
But it is the sun itself which produces the rays.
In fact, that glorious sun and its shining
Are one and the same.

To have a reflection, one must have an object;
If we see a reflection, then we infer that an object exists.
Likewise, the supreme reality, which is one,
Appears to be two.

2.7 "Everyday is today. There is no time or space in the reality."

It is not possible for the mind to understand that there is no time or space, because the process of thinking is itself based on time and space. Without first assuming the concepts of time and space, there is nothing to think about. Therefore, one has to assume a false position before one can even discuss time and space!

Many of the desires in our ordinary human life are directed towards the future. But where does that future exist? It is solely a mental construction, a fantasy. When tomorrow does materialize, it has already become today. Because we imagine a tomorrow and remember a yesterday, we always think we have time. However, time does not exist in reality, where concepts cannot reach.

In Vedanta, the test for reality is to enquire whether something is eternal (*nitya*) or whether it is bound by time. Eternal does not mean a very, very, very, long time, just as infinite does not mean very, very, very, big. It is the opposite or the negation of time. In eternity, there is no such thing as time. In the Self there is only pure existence that is always whole and complete and which never comes and goes. The rhythm of time in the gross world is kept by the breathing of the body, inhalation and exhalation, over and over again. But in that emptiness after one breath has gone out, and before the next breath is taken in, reality is always, already there.

2.8 "Power starts from zero, but reality is beyond."

Brahman in its original, unmanifest aspect is the reality. When *Brahman* becomes active, it manifests itself as *Maya*. The nature of *Maya* is zero—it doesn't really exist. So you have One (*Brahman*/reality) and zero (*Maya*). In Vedanta, *Brahman* plus *Maya* is called *Ishwara*, which Maharaj refers to as the power. (Note here that one plus zero is still one!) The power is free to create as many forms as it needs to satisfy its innate urge to expand indefinitely. To accomplish this, it creates beings with sense organs of increasing degrees of refinement. However, all the time that this is going on, the basis remains zero.

For this reason, nothing is permanent, everything is impermanent. Whatever appears, sooner or later has to return to the zero from which it appeared. For this reason, every experience is fleeting. Nothing can be held; it all slips away like water through the fingers. Nothing that the power creates is true, because it starts from zero. However, reality, *Brahman*, is One and it is *nitya*, eternal. It never comes and it never goes away.

2.9 "He is everywhere. He is not the body, and I am He."

What greater miracle is there than to be sitting here now, the body breathing effortlessly, and to know that you are alive? Life is everywhere; and sometimes you can feel your own power of consciousness enveloping everything that comes into awareness. The power that you feel energizes the body and fills it with the light of "I-amness." And yet that sense of "I-amness" is not focused on this apparent individual person—it goes far beyond that, into the limitless and timeless realm of pure knowledge, of universal consciousness. It is just one simple mistake that you make—to associate this limitless awareness with the limited and time-bound body. Nothing can limit the Self that you are, Its freedom is absolute. It is a freedom that has never known bondage.

"I am *Brahman*" is a phrase that is found in the Upanishads, where it is referred to as a *mahavakya* (great saying). Another *mahavakya* is "*tat tvam asi*" (you are That). Both sayings express the same truth. The concept that the *mahavakya* is communicating is not that "I," the individual, am "He," the underlying reality, taken as a whole. Obviously, you cannot fit the ocean into the wave! The concept is rather that what "I" am, when I recognize my true nature, is not different from that underlying reality. The wave is nothing but water. That is the meaning of "I am He."

2.10 "The base is true; I without I, but it doesn't speak."

There are four levels of speech, beginning with the *mahakarana* body, in which pure knowledge of existence provides the basis for all the thoughts that arise through the three lower bodies. That base is true—you can never deny your own existence. However, that existence is free from the veiling effect of ignorance, which means that there is no longer an identification between the "I" and the sense of physically limited and time-bound ego. That illusion is not there at this level. The pure knowledge is there as a base ("I without I"), but there are no concepts or thoughts, so that consciousness does not speak.

2.11 "What is true? Self without self."

The word "Self," like the word "I," points back to the one who is uttering it. It is a "reflexive" word, one that indicates the eternal subject, rather than one of Its objects. The real owner of the word Self is the One who is always present, the very essence of reality, reality Itself. It is a very sacred word and receives an upper case letter "S." On the other hand, the small ego-self receives a lower-case letter "s" to indicate its insignificance. It is rebuffed, dismissed as the impostor it is. This fraudulent self robs you of your birthright, which is to know yourself as you truly are, the universal and ever-free Self of all.

2.12 "I am everywhere and nothing else is there at all."

The mind doesn't understand Oneness for a long time. When it does finally understand it, it becomes quiet and ceases to hold onto the concept of multiple selves. Maharaj here says that "I am everywhere," pointing out that your own Self is the Self of all. There is no second Self. Understanding you are everywhere does not mean that you suddenly get the magical power to see through someone else's eyeballs. It means that you no longer conceive of the separate existence of "someone else." Rather, existence is One, and that is experienced as your own being; that is, as "I," the subject. Consciousness sees itself as the world.

2.13 "I am not the body. The body is a neighbor."

The source of awareness cannot be found anywhere within the body. The body is an object of that awareness in the same way that your next-door neighbor is an object of that awareness. There is no reason why you should not be friendly to this body while you find yourself living in close association with it. However, do not take it to be yourself. Its troubles are not your troubles. One day, when its time comes, the body will go, without asking your permission, in the same way that it appeared. It is necessary to have a human birth to get this knowledge from a Master, so it is best to uphold a grateful attitude and make use of the body for the sake of Self-knowledge.

2.14 "Everything is for the good."

The mind cannot grasp this statement by itself because it is really a declaration of the way life is felt beyond the mind. There has to be an intuitive understanding. There is a perfection in that state that can be felt but cannot be explained in words. Everything is for the good. Yes, that is how it is. However, repeating this truth to others who are experiencing suffering would be foolish and inconsiderate. There is no logical reason for the feeling that a realized person has that everything is for the good. That understanding is just there, and the nature of that understanding is emotional, not just intellectual. To know the Self is to know goodness at first hand, as the very essence of life.

2.15 "I never change. Circumstances change."

The awareness that you had when you were one year old and when you were 18 years old is exactly the same as the awareness that you have now. You are that pure and limitless awareness. When you know this beyond any doubt, you are free from the bondage of changing circumstances. Everything that is not true, that is illusion, changes. The "I" that is there one minute is not the same as the "I" that is there the next minute. There is a multiplicity of different "I's" in the human personality, and they emerge and dissolve in an ever-changing pattern, according to the stimuli of changing circumstances. They are all based on the false concept of "I" as a separate individual, which is called the ego. The ego remains from one day to the next as a kind of focus for the personality, but it is really nothing but a wrong belief or assumption. Only the constant background of awareness has real, permanent existence.

2.16 "Good or bad, everyone is myself."

Everyone has a concept about who is a good person and who is a bad person, but these concepts have no basis in reality. However "bad" you may think a person is, you can be sure that that person thinks of his actions as good. That person may be a murderer, but he is only doing what he is compelled to do and is really not "doing" anything. The saint may bless you and give you knowledge, but he is not "doing" anything either. The divine power gives to all alike the fruits of their past actions. *Papa* (wrong actions) and *punya* (right actions) must bear their fruit. Even the realized person has to experience in body and mind the results of actions already set into motion (*prarabdha karma*).

These immutable laws apply to the illusory level of the individual person, but they do not apply to the Self. Good and bad actions in a dream appear real at the time, but when I wake up, I know I have done nothing. In the same way, the good and bad characters in my dream were none other than myself.

2.17 "Final reality has no knowledge and no ignorance."

Maharaj would often use the phrase "final reality," rather than just "reality," to indicate that one's true nature is a step beyond knowledge as well as beyond ignorance. Jnaneshwar, in the *Amritanubhav,* wrote:

Fire, in the process of annihilating camphor,
Annihilates itself as well.
This is exactly what happens to knowledge
In the process of destroying ignorance.

When knowledge of the Self comes, the darkness of ignorance is no longer there. The false knowledge of "I am the body and the mind" is replaced by the correct knowledge "I am He, the reality." However, that knowledge is not the same thing as the reality itself. Knowledge can only be of some thing, which becomes the object of knowledge. This can never happen to the Self, which always remains beyond objectification, and so remains beyond knowledge.

The phrase "Self-knowledge" is not literally true, because the Self cannot be known. What it really means is that there is the knowledge that one is, and always has been, the final reality. Every aspirant has to come to this point. Knowledge from the Master can take you up to the door, but you have to go in and take ownership of the house yourself. Then there is no need to say "I am He, I am *Brahman*" (which is knowledge). You remain at home in your Self, without effort.

2.18 "Do not try to find reality, to recall it, for it is always there."

Understanding is really everything on the "way" that Maharaj taught. There is absolutely nothing to gain, because you are always already your Self, the final reality. To try to find reality is to behave like the man who went into a police station and reported that he had lost himself. The one who says "I am lost" is He. The Self doesn't need to remember Itself and the Self cannot forget Itself either. The mind remembers and forgets, but you are not the mind. What you are is always present; you only have to recognize it. You are the one who is looking, you are the one who is seeking. There is a Chinese verse:

A dunce went out looking for fire with a lighted lantern.
Had he known what fire was,
He could have cooked his rice much sooner.

2.19 "Reality is myself."

To find a cup in the dark, you need eyes and a lamp, but to find a lamp in the dark, you only need eyes, you don't need a lamp. Reality is self-evident, self-illuminating. You don't need anything external to find it, because it is already what you are. When Self-knowledge occurs, it becomes very clear to you that you and reality are one and the same, and that your nature is bright and pure like a flame that is always burning.

2.20 "I am always free (a free bird)."

The freedom that one has in reality does not come from liberation from bondage. It is a freedom that has never known bondage and so can hardly be called freedom. It feels like freedom to the one who believed he or she was bound but in fact it was there all the time and has only been recognized. The realized person says "I am always free and you are always free also." This freedom does not refer to freedom of action but to a freedom that has never performed any action and so is not constrained to receive the fruits of those actions. This freedom of the Self is like the freedom of the bird that can fly unhindered above the crawling and walking creatures of the earth.

2.21 "When the package is opened, the package doesn't remain."

The package that Maharaj is referring to with this analogy is the body-mind-ego. This package is a bundling together of different parts and functions, including the sense organs, the power of perception, the intellect, emotions, and so on. The making of this package is the inevitable result of the birth of the body and the mind. The package can be unwrapped or opened in two ways: by the death of the body mind or by self-enquiry. Through self-enquiry, the package is seen to be untrue; that is, it is understood that the so-called individual person is nothing but a concept. When you remove the string and paper that is binding the package together, what happens to the package? It is no longer there. In the same way, the concept "I exist" is the string and paper that holds together the package of the individual person. Remove it, and the illusion of the individual person is gone.

2.22 "One should just be and forget this and that."

Being is one of the characteristics or qualities of *Brahman* in the traditional description *sat-chit-ananda*. The word "*sat*" is often translated as "being." In this three-fold description, being is not different from "*chit*," which means "knowledge" or "consciousness," and not different from "*ananda*," which means fullness or completeness. To know oneself—to have Self-knowledge—means also to *be* oneself. Being is the most real experience one can have because it means also to be knowledge itself, the reality. But what is being? Being (*sat*) is that which is present now, which always has been present, and which always will be present. It is experienced as a stillness that is also pure knowledge and the feeling of satisfaction as well.

The *sat-chit-ananda* triad unites the three realms of physical body, intellect, and emotion which come together as understanding. As an aspirant, you may find that your path is marked by an increasing frequency of experiences of this kind of understanding and less and less disturbance from mundane concerns, which Maharaj here calls "this and that."

2.23 "Do anything, but understand where reality is. When you feel nothing, it is there."

"Do anything" in this context, should not be understood from the point of view of an imaginary "doer," but with the knowledge that it is the divine power that does everything, as in "He is doing everything." If you understand that power as the real doer, you may continue to play a part but you will not "feel" anything; that is, you do not feel that it is "I" who am acting. The feeling of "I am the doer" is one side of the coin and the feeling that "He is doing everything" is the other— they can't both be there at the same time.

2.24 "One who understands it is not true, is true."

Jnaneshwar, in the *Amritanubhav,* writes:

If the extinguisher of a light
Were extinguished along with the light,
Who would know that there was no light?

He who perceives that there is nothing
Does not himself become nothing.
The Self has this same unique kind of existence,
Beyond both existence and non-existence.

Awareness can never die. There is no way that awareness can ever be negated because there would always have to be awareness there to register that negation. There has to be a final reality that can say "there is nothing but me." Everything that happens can only happen because that awareness is there. However, the reverse is not true. That awareness does not require any of those events to happen—it remains just as it is without them. It is the same whether there is any object or not. It is unaffected by the appearance or existence of the world or by the disappearance of that world. That is the nature of the freedom of reality, and that is what makes it *nitya* (eternal).

2.25 "You, yourself, is effortless."

In the story of the *Ramayana, Rama* (the one who plays in everybody), after destroying the demon *Ravana* (the ego) regains his wife *Sita* (peace) and returns home to the city of *Ayodhya* (effortlessness). The natural state is effortless. That is what "natural" means—to be as one is without stress and strain. The Self is effortlessly natural because it does not participate at all in the play of the world. Self-knowledge brings a sense of effortlessness to the mind, which is a great relief after the efforts that were made to seek that Self. The constant demands of the ego go away and the mind settles into a state of peace, knowing that what has to be done has now been done.

2.26 "If you want to be something, it's a stamp of the ego and you remain in a state. Be nothing and reality remains."

There is no individual person anywhere. There is no one to be anything. That false assumption that "I am someone and I have to be something" is the essence of the ego. Who is it who wants to be something? To have the concept of being something, there has to first be the concept that the world is true as a ground in which "I" can be or become something. To live like this is to live in a state of ignorance. It is like becoming deeply involved in a dream and struggling to achieve a particular result, only to find that, on awakening, there is nothing there at all.

What does it mean to "be nothing?" It means to rest in your true nature and not let the mind go outward in pursuit of worldly goals. Reality remains before, during, and after the long dream of life. Even now you are That.

2.27 "The screen never says 'Oh, they're showing a bad picture. I won't show."

One of the commonest questions that comes up is: "Why did God create a world with so much suffering in it?" Few people stop to consider whether there is anything wrong with the question—it is taken for granted that there is an intelligence "in charge" of the whole show and that He is therefore responsible for everything that happens. You do not find this point of view in the *Upanishads* or in the teaching of *Advaita Vedanta*. You *do* find the positive affirmation that freedom from suffering can be found, and that it is in fact our birthright. However, it is also stated very clearly that freedom is to be found only in the realization that our true nature is unborn and undying.

The concept that the world should be free of suffering arises from identification with the body. Because the body is attracted to pleasure and repelled by pain, the ignorant mind simply reflects those opposites in its thinking. It labors under the illusion that the world can be made perfect, given sufficient time and effort. But when it is realized that the body is a transitory object that appears as if in a dream, it is no longer possible to imagine that real effects can follow from what it apparently does. If you kill someone in a dream, will you have to stand trial when you wake up? Is the screen responsible for the violence that takes place in the movie? In this way, God provides the power or life force for the whole play, but does not have any knowledge of, and consequently has no responsibility for, what happens in it.

2.28 "Reality has nothing to do with the world that has come up."

As long as you take it to be true, this world is bound to be confusing and difficult. You could say that it is designed to fail. It is not possible to find happiness in material or wordly objects. Efforts to do so always come to nothing in the end. Sooner or later, everyone comes to the conclusion that the solution to the problems of living have to lie in some other direction altogether. In this sense, everyone is a seeker after truth. Some know it and consciously follow a spiritual path while others are still in a process of becoming disillusioned.

All this seeking and all the different levels of understanding that seekers reach plays itself out within this closed system, this "box" called the world. It is a closed system because the belief that the world is true is what maintains it. The seeker's belief in his or her own reality and the notion that he or she has to do something to escape are all part of the system that keeps them firmly locked in the box. Reality itself is unaffected by what goes on within this closed system.

2.29 "In the final reality, there is nothing to understand."

Understanding the nature of reality is a process that everyone has to go through on the way to liberation. Ironically, when that liberation comes, it is understood that there is nothing to understand. You are the reality, pure and simple, and there is no ignorance to make you think otherwise, even for a moment. Where is the need for understanding? Reality just is; it is self-evident. There is Oneness, and so there is no one to understand, no object of understanding, and no experience of understanding. It is natural that understanding grows and deepens all the time that you are an aspirant, but when "final understanding" of reality comes, understanding itself is seen as not true, because it belongs to the mind.

3

March: The Dreamer and the Dream

3.1 "I am the creator of the world."

Just as the spider spins its web out of its own body so the ego projects the world of separate objects on the unchanging background of reality. The creator of the world is the "I." The "I" is not there in deep sleep and so no world appears. This is symbolized in Hindu mythology in the following way. The god *Vishnu*, who represents the Absolute, is sleeping on the vast and dark cosmic ocean. While he is sleeping, a lotus emerges from his navel and in the center of that lotus sits the god *Brahma*, who is the creator. This signifies that the Absolute reality does not create anything directly. However, within that reality, the I-thought appears, which in turn gives rise to the appearance of the world.

3.2 "Everything I see or perceive is only a dream."

Comparing the waking state with the dream state is extremely useful in explaining the nature of reality. It has been said that it is only because we know and recognize the dream state that we have the possibility of understanding that this waking state, which seems so real, is also nothing but a dream. The key point about the dream state, which nobody ever doubts, is that the whole of the dream world and the dream experience is contained within me, the dreamer. When I wake up, I know this as a fact. Because of this fact, I am willing to consider the possibility that I am dreaming this world in the so-called waking state as well.

How does a dream work? There is a state of deep sleep and in that sleep a thought comes in the form of the consciousness: "I am." This thought is like a light bulb. Stored experiences then unravel in associative patterns, moving in front of the light of the I-thought, and pictures, thoughts, sensations, and emotions appear. There is even the sense of being the actor, the "doer" in the dream. All the time though, the person who is dreaming is sound asleep in bed somewhere. Exactly the same thing happens in the waking state. Everything that appears in it is simply a more vivid and (usually), more rational dream image.

3.3 "Birth means the picture on the TV screen comes on; death, it goes off."

In order for there to be a picture on the TV screen, there has to be an electric current, and the set has to be switched on. In the same way, the body is conceived, formed, and born. Then, somewhat later, thoughts form in the mind of the infant. The power of universal consciousness makes the whole process work. Conception, growth, birth, mental development through accumulation and processing of sense impressions—all these processes happen because the power is always there. There is a continuous cycle of birth, death, conception, and rebirth, all of which happens in the presence of the Self.

In the West, birth, for astrological purposes, is defined as the moment when the body of the child emerges from the mother's body into the outside world and takes its first independent breath. In the same way, death is taken to be the moment when the physical body stops breathing and the heart stops beating. These may be convenient and practical definitions, but who or what is really born?

Maharaj teaches that no one is really born and no one dies. The birth of the imaginary individual person occurs when the first concept "I exist" appears. At that moment, the TV set is switched on. Then, once that first tiny surge of electricity charges up the circuits, the picture show of individual self, other selves, and the whole world appears on the screen. "Death" of this picture show comes when the set is switched off. This may actually occur after the death of the physical body, because death really means the dissolution of the sense of the individual "person." Sooner or later, though, this happens, and the cycle continues; that is to say, another TV set picks up the signal somewhere else. However, the "person" is not reborn, because that person was limited to that particular TV set, which has now been permanently switched off.

3.4 "When I go to the source of myself, I disappear."

If you travel along a river and follow it to its source, it becomes more and more attenuated until finally, at the source itself, it disappears altogether. This analogy is similar to the one about the tree growing from the seed, in that it indicates that the same natural process of growth is responsible for the appearance of the illusory separate self and its world. The first trickle of water, like the first surge of electricity, or the sprouting of the seed, point to the emergence of knowledge from ignorance, which in turn happens against the unchanging background of awareness. To return to the source means to become absorbed by the power of reality, to lose the sense of individuality in that Oneness. When that happens, *you* remain there as existence itself, but without the separate "I."

3.5 "Feel that you are the creator of the world, and that you can also destroy it."

Why does Maharaj say "Feel that you can also destroy the world?" He wants you to acknowledge and feel your own power. The world is nothing but your own thought. You can destroy it simply by forgetting about it, as, for example, when you go to sleep. There is no need to destroy the world—why destroy what is not true?—but there is a need to accept your power in relation to it and to understand that you are the one that the world depends on for its existence. So by all means feel that it is yours to destroy and to create.

3.6 "What I have created is not true."

Looking back on it, you never believe that the dream that you had last night was true, even though while that dream was going on, you never imagined that it was not true. You readily acknowledge that all the events of the dream were going on while you, yourself, were sleeping in your bed. The whole thing appeared but you were not really involved in it at all.

This waking state is also a dream and it is not true, for exactly the same reasons. Dreaming is a spontaneous process that creates a world out of the material springing forth from the mind. How is this waking dream different from the sleeping dream? It goes on by itself. The Self never makes any comment about it.

3.7 "I am not doing anything at all."

We are so used to thinking of "I" as the doer, as in "I am reading," "I am sitting," "I am trying to understand," that a statement such as this one seems to make no sense at all. However, Maharaj was not speaking from the point of view of an individual "I," or person, but from the point of view of the Self; or what he sometimes called "I without I." That Self is the real subject of the first-person pronoun. Whenever you say "I," you are referring to that ocean of pure consciousness, whether you know it or not. In the state of ignorance, however, "I" means the imaginary individual "doer" and you remain asleep to yourself as reality. In fact, "I" is a sacred word, just as "Self" is a sacred word. The ocean does not "do" anything to create the waves that appear on its surface, neither does the dreamer do anything to create the dream that appears.

3.8 "Nothing is true. In a dream, I've seen, but I've not seen."

In a dream, something really quite miraculous occurs; you see with closed eyes! When you awake, however, the mystery is solved, and you dismiss the whole business—it was just a dream. Everything that you saw in the dream was only a projection of the mind on the screen of awareness. Awareness itself did not participate in the dream events but it provided the background for the images to appear. On awakening from sleep, the images and objects of the waking state displace those of the dream state. The dream disappears. What has happened to awareness? Nothing has happened to it. It continues to provide the same, unchanging background for whatever happens in the waking state. Later, when you go to sleep at night, the dream world starts up again, displacing the waking state. Awareness is not affected by this change either but remains as the background. "Seeing" occurs, both in the dream state and in the waking state, but "I," the awareness, does not see anything at all.

3.9 "Don't be an ant, be a lion, and say "No death for me!"

Death is really only a concept. It has power because we give power to it. As long as we take ourselves to be small and insignificant individuals, we are subject to the fear of death. Our view of life is mistaken. We imagine ourselves to be subject to appearance and disappearance and we forget that for something to appear and disappear, a changeless background is necessary. Just as a river flowing to the sea is water when it begins as a tiny spring, is water when it passes through the country, and is still water when it merges into the vast ocean, so are we pure consciousness before "birth," pure consciousness during this life, and pure consciousness after "death."

3.10 "Desire for something better has made me take birth again and again."

Maharaj took it for granted that rebirth is a fact for the individual person or *jiva*. The *jiva* is a "bundle" made up of the subtle body (mind), the sense of doership, and the "I"-thought, or ego. It is the *jiva* that harbors various desires and it is these desires that make the *jiva* go from one body to another. The *jiva* is restless because its desires are never completely satisfied—as soon as one desire is fulfilled, another one appears to take its place. The *jiva* appears in one life and then another in its attempts to find satisfaction. This movement continues until Self-knowledge dawns with the help of a true teacher (*sadguru*).

Self-knowledge destroys the false sense of "I" (*ahamkara*) and leaves the *jiva* free from the pressure of the unfulfilled desires. The *jiva* is then called *jivanmukta*; one who is liberated while living. The *jivan-mukta* does not have to continue the cycle of birth and rebirth because there is no center of unfulfilled desire to prompt any further birth. Death of the *jivanmukta*'s body puts an end to the movement once and for all and brings rest. This is what the *Upanishads* and the other scriptures of India say.

3.11 "The world is nothing but a long dream."

Who is the dreamer of the dream of the world? The one who is sleeping is the dreamer. The one who appears as a character in the dream is not the dreamer. The character in the dream has no control over what happens; the dream unfolds spontaneously by itself. This character imagines that its "life" starts at "birth" and ends at "death," and is a continuous experience, apart from interruptions at regular intervals by the states of dream, which it regards as unreal, and deep sleep, which it regards as its own absence.

This is all fantasy. The character is part of the dream. The whole span of "life," with the alternation of the three states of waking, dreaming, and deep sleep, is a long dream for one who is "awake" to the reality.

3.12 "The whole world is nothing but His shadow."

The world is an infinitely complex layering and structuring of inert matter illuminated by the presence of the Self. The Self is everywhere, as is said in the *Brihadaranyaka Upanishad*:

As a razor in its case or as fire in wood, so dwells the Self, the Lord of the universe in all forms, even to the tips of the fingers.

The living beings of the world follow the Self like the shadow follows the man as he walks. When the power of the Self is there, the body lives. When it departs, the body dies. The relationship is one of total dependence. But the beauty of the Self is that it is always already there. He is the One who is living in this body, and He is always free and independent of it.

3.13 "I don't do anything. The body does it."

If, in the evening, you look back on the events of the day, you see how many different things you appeared to do during those hours. You seemed to be acting consciously, though sometimes you can distinguish actions that happened completely mechanically, without thinking, from other actions that required some thought or preparation. Whatever the actions were, you are still here, remembering them. Although you may not have been aware of it at the time, you were also there when any of those actions were taking place. You remain always, whatever experiences come and go, as the witness of those events. The body does the actions, prompted by the mind, but you are not affected by them because you are unchanging. Identification with the body makes you believe that the actions are your actions. That freedom from action is already yours, you only have to realize it.

3.14 "Free will means no bondage."

The ego imagines that free will means the freedom to do whatever it wants. This seems desirable because it knows intuitively that it doesn't have that freedom now. The seeker understands that there is bondage, but may not understand that it is because of the "I" concept. He or she imagines that liberation will somehow bring about that freedom of action. That concept of unconstrained action is still there. But the realized person does not operate on that basis. For him or her free will means harmony with what is, as it is. If that were not so; that is, if such a person were not able to accept whatever happened, then he or she would not be free at all. So free will means liberation from the bondage of the ego, which is based on the false concept that "I" am the doer. When that concept of doership is gone, the question of free will does not arise.

3.15 "'I don't exist.' That is the real free will."

The concept of free will is really something of a joke. In the West, it is often regarded as axiomatic; certainly it is enshrined in Christian dogma. On the other hand, in the Sanskrit language, and in the Indian languages derived from it, there is no word for free will. The concept just doesn't exist. It is taken for granted that everything happens as a manifestation of divine law. Maharaj is therefore being rather playful here, when he says that the real free will comes when there is the understanding "I don't exist." He is pointing out that in reality, there is nothing like free will. The concept only arises in ignorance, because of the notion that "I am the doer." Choice exists as long as you imagine that you are doing something, but if there is no concept of doership, then there is no concept of free will either.

3.16 "Tomorrow never comes."

It is always now, whether you are remembering the past or speculating about the future. Memory is only a thought in this moment and so is speculation. The concepts of past and future are false because they have no substance—the supposed objects that the words indicate do not exist. The only reality is that which does exist, and to exist means that it cannot not exist. Non-existence is also only a concept that does not refer to anything real. There cannot be any such thing, by definition. Eternity is that which is here now and that is the Self.

3.17 "He does everything for you. Don't worry, He is in everybody."

In November 2000, the Self in the form of Maharaj put aside the limitation of that human body and became the everything that it already was. Now, when I look at his picture, I feel him everywhere. When he was in the body, Maharaj would refer to his Master as the divine power, and would say things like "What a beautiful day my Master has provided!" God has many names, but to conceive of Him as one's own Master is perhaps most effective for the devotee because it is so personal. However the Divine power is conceived, He is always endowed with the same attributes of omniscience, omnipresence, and omnipotence. Some devotees may look upon their God with awe and even fear, but those who consider their guru to be God are the most fortunate, because they always look upon Him with pure love and gratitude.

3.18 "I have spoken so many words. Where are they now? Where have they gone?"

Like actors emerging from the wings at the side of the stage, speaking their lines, and then returning behind the curtain, thoughts emerge from nothingness, formulate themselves in the mind, and then disappear again into nothingness. So many words spoken and all of them come to nothing! When you contemplate this constant materialization and dematerialization, the dreamlike quality of life becomes apparent. We do not know where thoughts come from, or, to put it another way, thoughts come from not-knowing. Before a thought is remembered, it must be forgotten. Forgetfulness or not-knowing is pure ignorance. Therefore thought, knowledge, comes from ignorance and returns to ignorance. Reality does not have any ignorance and it does not have any knowledge either. Jnaneshwar wrote in the *Amritanubhav*:

The Sun does not know the night;
But can He know when it is day?
In the same way, the one Being
Is without the ability to remember or forget.

3.19 "Whatever you do is nothing anyway, so do nothing."

Why do we act in the world, rushing around trying to accomplish this or that? Because we take it to be true. But what if it becomes clear that it is all a dream? That dream may continue, but as long as you see it as a dream and nothing else, what will you try to accomplish? It would be absurd to try to do anything. If you are awake to the dream, everything is nothing.

3.20 "When emotion or thought come in your mind, understand that you do nothing and the "I" doesn't exist."

The dream character cannot do anything, neither does the "I" that appears to be the doer really exist. No one can have any idea what thought or emotion is going to pop up next. In the end, you find that you cannot take such a dream-life seriously.

For the aspirant, however, separating from the thoughts and emotions that arise becomes a way of life. The thoughts and emotions that it is most important to separate from are the ones that cause emotional disturbance, for example, negative emotions such as anger or fear. When there is an emotional disturbance, the mind cannot reflect the Self clearly.

In its natural state, the mind has no thoughts in particular, and no violent attractions or repulsions disturb its equilibrium. Consequently, the Self is felt clearly, like sunlight on still water. As an aspirant, it is still possible to have a relatively peaceful mind by avoiding strong desires and emotions and separating the real existence as pure being from the false idea that "I" exist as the "doer."

3.21 "The world is a game, nothing else. Play with this understanding."

The world can only really be enjoyed when it is understood that it is nothing. When you know that the world is not true, then certainly it becomes a game for you. When you are playing a game, in the spirit of a game, you are always aware that there are no real consequences. What makes the world seem so serious and stressful is the wrong assumption that it is all real. The result is struggle and competition, and the feeling that one is playing for high stakes. Someone like Maharaj, on the other hand, does not see the world as having real, independent existence and so plays in it like a child playing a game, just for fun. There is no concern about losing and no desire to win because there is no sense of being in a competition. Life, seen in the light of the Self, is not for achievement, but for play.

3.22 "It is always for something which doesn't exist that you must do something."

If something is real and exists, then it always exists, it cannot not exist. It has being. It is never necessary to do anything for being to be, for existence to exist. Its very nature is to be and to exist. The corollary of this statement is that that which is not true has no being; it cannot and does not exist. One way that you can tell something is not true is that it is not permanent; it comes and goes, and yet it is precisely for these kind of objects that many people struggle for a whole lifetime. When you think of "doing" something, acquiring something considered desirable, or accomplishing something considered valuable, you are in fact directing your efforts towards nothing.

Self-knowledge, which you might imagine to be the greatest acquisition, is in fact not an acquisition at all. Nothing can be done to attain it, because you already are the Self. The "knowledge" in Self-knowledge is really only the disappearance of the veil of ignorance that prevents you from seeing what is already there.

3.23 "Everything happens."

If you take yourself to be an individual, you cannot understand that everything happens. There is no "doer" anywhere, but as long as you takes yourself to be a person, you remain the "doer." If this is the case, it is surely best to be honest and accept that you are still in illusion and that you have an apparent problem, which is that you do not feel complete. In that situation, it is right and appropriate to accept the longing to be complete as a way of life—that is what "aspirant" means. Then grace can come and the problem can be resolved.

An idea such as "everything happens" can be very confusing if it is overemphasized. You may come to believe that you have no power. Some aspirants lapse into a kind of fatalistic attitude, in which they essentially give up their hopes. It is best to persist in whatever practice you are doing and consistently apply what the Master says. Realize the Self first, and then you can honestly say "Everything happens."

3.24 "As long as I is there, it's a dream."

The mind is *Maya*. The I is the root of the illusion. When the I is not there in deep sleep, there is no dream and no world. The ego is always there in the waking state. The realized person sees the same world because the I is still there. However the realized person sees the long dream of life as a dream and does not take it to be true.

3.25 "Unless you sleep, how can you get the dream? So, unless you forget yourself, how can the world be produced?"

Just as nobody goes without sleep, so nobody avoids forgetting reality. When did we first forget our true nature? When did that ignorance begin? Who can say? All that we know is that ignorance is there, and in that forgetfulness, the illusion of the world of separate objects has appeared. Ignorance (*Maya*) is therefore considered to be beginingless in Vedanta, although it does have an end. That end comes when you awaken from the dream of individuality into the light of Self-knowledge.

3.26 "From knowledge everything happens. Knowledge is the creator."

The creator of the world, the Lord of the Universe, is nothing but knowledge itself. That knowledge is the very same knowledge "I am" that exists in all the objects of the creation, from *Brahma* to a blade of grass, as is said in the *Upanishads*. That power is the creative power that is always active, always in movement, building up new forms and causing them to act according to their inherent qualities. Everything happens on the basis of this knowledge. That knowledge is His power. It is everywhere, and you are That.

3.27 "All that you see and perceive is nothing but God's dream. It is the magic of God, and it's all wrong."

Before there is any creation, the divine remains unmanifest, resting in Oneness. In that profound sleep, a thought arises "I am." That thought is *Maya*, the manifestation of the power of *Brahman*. *Brahman* is no longer just *Parabrahman*, beyond duality, but becomes *Ishwara*, the Lord of the Universe, as well. From that division of one into two the whole dream of the world spreads itself out. Jnaneshwar describes this duality in terms of *Shiva* and *Shakti*, the God and the Goddess:

In unity, there is little to behold;
So She, the mother of abundance,
Brought forth the world as a play.

While He sleeps, She gives birth
To the animate and inanimate worlds.
When She rests,
Her Husband disappears.

3.28 "One should try to forget the knowledge. As you have got the knowledge, you are in sleep."

Knowledge creates a whole world, but that world has nothing to do with reality. That world springs from the thought "I exist." From that thought the individual person appears, and that person then has to shoulder all the problems and cares of a separate human existence. It is all nonsense! The individual person never existed. Knowledge is not some blessing but is the source of all the trouble. Knowledge arises from ignorance, just as a dream appears in sleep. To feel that you know yourself as an individual entity is to believe in a dream.

In the *Kena Upanishad* it is said:

He truly knows Brahman who knows him as beyond knowledge. He who thinks that he knows, knows not.

3.29 "Happiness lies in the forgetting of the world."

When you are deeply asleep, you have no problem at all with the world, whatever the circumstances of the waking state, because you forget about it altogether. Certainly, you are happy then, because there is no knowledge of the world. However, there is no knowledge of happiness either and so you cannot fully experience it. It is only when you return to the waking state that you say "I was happy (while I slept)." Your true nature is still veiled by ignorance during deep sleep. Real happiness is experienced when you realize the Self. The veil of ignorance falls away and the mind gains knowledge of the happiness and fullness that is its true nature.

3.30 "One who remains on the surface is carried away in the stream of pleasure and suffering."

The world is not a place in which lasting pleasure can be gained. In fact, the expression "lasting pleasure" is a contradiction. However much time people spend trying to enjoy themselves, the process is inherently frustrating. The world always fools them in the end. The pursuit of pleasure and the avoidance of suffering makes life into a constant struggle, a pattern of resistance, desire, and denial. This disturbance is like the constantly swirling water on the surface of a flowing river. A person caught in this current rarely has the chance to reflect on his or her true nature and being. For a pure reflection, and for understanding, the mind must be clear and still.

3.31 "Death is nothing. There is no death for anybody."

In deep sleep, a dream begins. Where was the dreamer before the dream began? The dreamer dreams the dream and then stops dreaming, returning to the state of deep sleep. Where has the dreamer gone?

Before "birth," where were you? During "life," where are you? After "death," where will you be?

Death is nothing. There is no death for anybody because nobody is ever born. Life is all a dream, an illusion, nothing but thought. The dreamer appears with the dream and disappears with it. Why should you be concerned with what appears and disappears? You remain always as the Absolute and final reality. Realize That and be free.

April: Knowledge and Ignorance

4.1 "Ignorance means nothing, zero."

What is ignorance? Ignorance means the Self not knowing Itself. Everything is the Self, so ignorance is also the Self; it is the "not-knowingness of the Self." It is like a veil that the Self draws over Itself. We cannot say that ignorance does not exist, because it has this veiling effect. Neither can we say that it does exist, because ignorance is a state of zero. Does zero exist? It is useful as a concept in mathematics and logic, but in itself it is nothing.

Ignorance is not opposed to ordinary knowledge, because the two can coexist; that is, there is knowledge of one's own existence and ignorance of one's true nature at the same time. The two: knowledge and ignorance, go together like twin brothers. What is ordinary knowledge then? Knowledge is the awareness of individual existence—"I am, and I am aware of it." This ego-knowledge is generally what Maharaj meant when he used the word "knowledge."

4.2 "Don't go back to ignorance. Ego is ignorance."

Once you have heard the Master's teaching and begun to accept it, don't leave it. Let that process of ripening come to fruition in you. You need time to reflect and meditate on what the Master has said, so that those thoughts can penetrate and in effect become your own thoughts. Don't go back to ignorance by imagining that you know best, that you can do anything by yourself, or that you can get liberation by any means other than whole-hearted commitment. This is all ego. The ego is the embodiment of ignorance. Don't resist the process that is happening. Hold fast to the knowledge given by the Master until it frees you absolutely.

4.3 "Be ignorant to the world and knowledgeable to the reality."

This is a very tidy and symmetrical sentence that puts knowledge and ignorance in the right perspective. The world, in the everyday sense of a collection of an infinite number of objects separate from "I," is itself the product of ignorance. That perception of the world is untrue, it does not retain its meaning for the person with Self knowledge. So ignorance, or forgetfulness, is appropriate with regard to that so-called world. Reality, on the other hand, is existence itself. To be knowledgeable to that reality is to be That. Real knowledge is Self-knowledge. Anything else is knowledge of something that does not exist.

4.4 "I am an ignorant person. I know that I know nothing."

Maharaj liked to refer to the well-known statement of Socrates, who came to the conclusion that he knew more than his contemporaries because he, at least, knew that he knew nothing, whereas they deluded themselves into believing that they were knowledgeable. If all you know relates to what doesn't exist, then what do you really know? If the "I" that you take yourself to be is itself not real, and that "I" is the knower, then how can "you" know anything? When these ideas penetrate and stay in the mind, then you become what Maharaj playfully refs to here as "an ignorant person." You are aware that the knowledge you had all amounted to nothing. Then you are ignorant in the right way. In fact, you have some real knowledge.

4.5 "Power is knowledge. Knowledge is power."

Power is the power of reality, the divine *Shakti*, or *Brahman*'s power of *Maya*. This power manifests as that knowledge or "I-amness" that all sentient beings experience. Before Self-realization occurs, this power of knowledge is perceived through the filter of the concept of individual "I" or ego. Essentially, the Self splits Itself into two: "I," and the power. The result is that there is a relative experience of reality. You perceive a reflection of reality, not the absolute reality itself. "I" is like the image of the sun reflected in a bucket of water. The bucket of water is the mind and its thoughts, so that the clarity of the reflection of reality is determined by the quality or purity of the thoughts. Hence the emphasis on purification of the mind in the philosophy and practice of yoga.

As long as you are an aspirant, you have this kind of relationship with the divine power. You may conceive of this power as God, in whatever form you wish, or you may consider the guru to be the embodiment of that power. However you conceive of it, the power always has the same divine attributes of omniscience, omnipotence, and omnipresence in relation to yourself, which you continue to consider as separate from that power. You worship the divine power and pray to it. In fact, this one power is the recipient of all the worship of all the devotees of all the diverse religions of the world.

As the mind becomes purified through practice (*sadhana*), you may have various kinds of experiences of closeness or union with this power. However, it remains separate because of the veil of ignorance. Finally, when the Self realizes Itself, you understand that the power is yourself, that there is no divine power apart from yourself, that you are that One that you were seeking, worshipping, and praying to. Then you become knowledge itself, and you are present in all beings, everywhere. That is Self-knowledge and that is the end of the search.

4.6 "The power doesn't know anything. Doesn't know "I'm power."

It is ironic that the God we are praying to does not know who we are, does not distinguish the saint from the sinner. Why? Because it is only a power—a tremendous, divine power that has the effect of drawing all creatures back to It as the source of everything—but It is not a knower. The individual human being is the knower, and the individual human being is an illusion. "We" do not exist as individuals because the whole process is the Self seeking Itself in order to unite with Itself.

The realization of that fact is not there during the search. What "we" are in reality is knowledge itself. That knowledge or power does not know any objects. Only the human mind knows objects. As humans, we project this kind of knowing onto the divine and so create a God in our own image. This is a comfortable point of view, but it is one which ultimately gets given up in the final understanding of the non-dual nature of reality.

4.7 "With that power I see. Power doesn't see."

"Seeing" occurs in the waking state. It is a physiological function, involving lenses and color filters, the nervous system, and the brain. All the senses operate in a similar fashion. The power makes them work, but the power does not see or hear, touch or taste. Electricity makes a computer work, but electricity does not produce the text on the screen or calculate the numbers. The computer's hardware and software does that.

4.8 "I am the power that is in the body."

Identification with the body makes you feel that the thoughts are "my" thoughts and that the sense perceptions are "my" perceptions. Actually the body and mind are lifeless. There is nobody there! There is no individual person. The so-called individual is only a concept of that inert body and mind. "I" actually refers to the power that happens to be in the body. This "I" is also everywhere else, giving life to all the bodies and all the minds. How can "I" be everywhere? "I" as an individual cannot, but that "I" has never existed. The real "I" has always been everywhere as the eternal subject. Only the concept of individual existence was wrong.

4.9 "Go to the root of the mind. Mind and knowledge do not remain."

If the Self does not have a concept of its own existence, then it essentially does not have a mind. That does not mean that the Self does not exist, only that there is no conceptualizing in it. The individual person and the whole world that appears to that individual are built out of concepts and are based on the fundamental concept "I am." One's very existence as a person is based on a concept. There is therefore a great fear of losing that concept, which is called the fear of death. All such problems arise from the identification of the Self with a concept. But that concept of individual existence arose for reasons that cannot be known to the individual mind, because the mind is itself a product of that arising. The Self was already there. That was your condition as an infant. You had no knowledge of your own existence. That knowledge was there only as a seed, as potential. It didn't bother to ask you if it was OK with you if it appeared and sprouted into a complete world-picture. Now that it has appeared and "you" have appeared along with it, "you" must return to that condition before the seed sprouted. Then, mind becomes no-mind and there is no longer any "you." The Self remains at peace, resting in Its true nature.

4.10 "The power is also not true."

If you look up at the sun, you feel its power as light and heat. That power is true for you. If you *are* the sun, you don't feel any light and heat. That power is not true for you. Maharaj is speaking here from the point of view of the sun, which symbolizes the Absolute reality.

4.11 "Knowledge is never satisfied. It wants to know more and more."

It is the nature of consciousness to create more and more forms, in order to have more and more experiences. Knowledge is like a power that makes everything run on and on. Living forms are born, experience according to their functions, and then die, only to be replaced by more complex forms with more refined functions that allow for more sophisticated experiences. So consciousness develops minerals, plants, animals, and finally human beings, "the crown of creation." Still the power continues, evolving more and more intelligence in the human being, gathering more and more information, more and more knowledge about what is not true in a constant search for happiness and fulfilment. When will it stop? Only when it receives real knowledge that explains its true nature as reality and it is able to accept and understand that knowledge. Then, at last, it ceases its movement and merges itself in its source.

4.12 "Doubt is ignorance, nothing else."

Self-knowledge that is beyond any doubt is a characteristic of a realized person, but as long as you are an aspirant, you cannot know with absolute conviction who you are. Therefore, you are subject to doubts, such as "How can I be reality?" Doubt is, in fact, nothing else than the absence of that knowledge of "Who am I?" Absence of Self-knowledge is therefore one definition of ignorance. Doubt is the very nature of the terrain that you are traversing on your way to Self-knowledge.

4.13 "I don't know anything. I know Him only."

The knowledge that you have is not "your" knowledge. You are knowledge itself and you don't have any knowledge of facts or things. The "real" knowledge that the Master gives has the purpose of breaking the identification with the body and making you realize yourself as universal consciousness, as "He." You are He, and you know yourself by being yourself. Then you can say "I don't know anything. I know

Him only." All other knowledge is false and, at best, of temporary usefulness.

4.14 "When I want something more, I have forgotten myself."

Why do we want something? Because we think that object will make us happy. Why do we think like that? Because we have forgotten that we are already happiness itself, that happiness and completeness is our true nature as reality. It may seem strange to see the word "forgotten" used here, because it may seem that reality has never been known. However, that is not true. You do know your true nature all the time because you *are* that reality. Forgetting means ignorance. As long as ignorance remains, it acts as a veil to keep reality unknown. All the moments of happiness and fullness that you do have are made possible by the temporary disappearance of the ignorance that is embodied as the ego. Naturally, you seek more of these experiences, until, eventually, you come to understand the reality behind them. Then you are satisfied with That.

4.15 "Do things, anything, no harm, but do not forget yourself."

If you are an actor in a play, you do everything written for your character to do, but you don't forget yourself and mix yourself up with the character. You may kill or be killed in the play but you still know that your wife or husband is sleeping soundly in bed at home. This statement from Maharaj is not an exhortation to make some kind of effort to "remember yourself" in the sense of "being in the moment" and so on. Anything that can be remembered or forgotten cannot be real. This is really a statement about *Karma yoga*, like those in the *Bhagavad Gita*. As an aspirant, when you perform actions, if you remember that the divine power is doing everything for you, you will develop devotion and the ego will be weakened. Later, you understand that the actions have always been performed by that power without there ever having been any "doer."

4.16 "Reality has no duty."

Electricity has no obligation to the appliances that it supplies with power. A human being may have many notions about God's responsibilities and duties but they are only the result of wishful thinking. Man's God often wears a human face and has human traits and human failings. Such a God is expected to indulge his devotees by fulfilling their desires. In fact, God has no duty. Great faith may result in a divine vision, but it is the power of faith that produces it and it is not God's obligation to respond. The power remains as power. It makes everything happen, but it does not take part in the drama.

4.17 "I am only a thought, and thought is wrong."

Self-realization or enlightenment is actually a very simple thing, really nothing special. The only thing that happens is that a wrong concept goes off. What is that wrong concept? The concept that there was somebody there who had something to gain. The spiritual search ends with the understanding that there is nobody to understand. "I," the one who was seeking, was only a thought. All thought was wrong that was based on that illusion. "I" actually refers to the One who was being sought. It was the Self seeking Itself all along. Now it knows Itself as the subject.

4.18 "You have to go beyond zero. You have to go beyond the space."

Mere absence of thought does not put you into reality. Thought is the subtle body and absence of thought is the causal body, which is a state of pure ignorance, or zero. When there is no thought, you simply don't know anything. You are not self-aware. It is the same as being deeply asleep. The causal body is like a gap between the world of objects and the Self. You have to go beyond zero, beyond space, to realize the Self. Space is more subtle than objects because it pervades them, objects appear in space. It is more subtle than thought, for the same reason. However, you, as pure awareness, are subtler than space. You pervade it. You are aware of it. It appears in your awareness.

When you realize that you are the One who is aware even of the zero-space, in which there is nothing, then you have reached the *mahakarana*, or supra-causal, body. The characteristic of this body is that consciousness is self-evident. It shines by its own light. This condition is described in the *Mandukya Upanishad*, where it is called The Fourth, because it is beyond the three states of waking, dreaming, and deep sleep.

The Fourth, the Self, is OM, the indivisible syllable. This syllable is unutterable, and beyond mind. In it the manifold universe disappears. It is the supreme good— One without a second. Whosoever knows OM, the Self, becomes the Self.

4.19 "Be out of your thoughts and then you can understand the reality."

True being is beyond the level of thought, and beyond the level of absence of thought. Meditation is extremely useful for coming to this understanding. In meditation, using the mantra given by the Master, you can cross the sea of thoughts and arrive at the calm harbor of the causal body. From here, it is only a step to reach the shore of the Self. Through meditation, initial understanding and experience of one's true being comes in a conscious way. It puts thoughts into perspective, so that you find yourself better able to be out of them during the ordinary circumstances of life as well.

4.20 "Understand I am the root of happiness and the ego is the root of unhappiness."

It is the most extraordinary and inexplicable irony that you are happiness yourself and yet, because you do not realize it, you seek for it outside. The happiness (*ananda*) that you naturally are, if you only knew it, is the ultimate happiness—a joy and fullness that never changes and is never diminished. What else could you possibly want? And yet even sincere seekers cannot accept that this happiness is already theirs. They continue to entertain doubts about that final understanding.

Often, the ego takes the blame, as though the ego were some powerful demon that had its own strength and its own will. The ego is the source of unhappiness, yes, but you only give it greater strength by believing in its power. In fact, it has no power. It is a false God, the false "I" that is born out of ignorance of reality. Reality is the true "I," the existence that you already know as Being and as happiness itself.

4.21 "Knowledge should increase so it can understand "Myself is wrong."

The knowledge that the Master gives will take you beyond all thought, if you allow it. First, that knowledge has to increase. which means that it changes your concept of who you are. On the way of knowledge (*jnana yoga*), the mind becomes bigger and bigger so that you can understand "I am everything." At the same time, you understand that you are not the small, insignificant creature that you imagined ourself to be. That concept of yourself as a powerless individual, destined to die, is the vision of self that is wrong.

4.22 "Knowledge is a disease."

Reality is not a knower. The Self is there whether there is knowledge or not. Knowledge means awareness of existence. In the human form, it means the appearance of the "I" thought. This knowledge happened, just as, when you are sleeping, a dream happens. Knowledge comes and goes according to its own laws and principles, over which no one has any control. No individual exists to exercise control because the individual existence is itself contained within that knowledge. The cause of this disease is not known to the one who suffers from it. The sufferer is in fact a symptom of the disease!

4.23 "Don't know anything. Be out of knowingness. Then you are always with yourself."

Ordinary knowledge belongs to the mind and will disappear with the death of the body on which it depends. Self-knowledge is not knowledge in the ordinary sense. It occurs when the false sense of "I," which is based on ordinary knowledge, is surrendered. What remains is a different kind of knowledge, not one that is rooted in the mind, but one that is established beyond the mind. This "pure knowledge" is not separate from existence itself and is not separate from pure happiness and completeness. It is the "chit" aspect of the *sat-chit-ananda* triad. Pure knowledge, or Self-knowledge, means abiding in the Self because there is no difference between the Self and its knowledge. To know the Self is to be the Self. The *Brihadaranyaka Upanishad* says:

Brahman can be apprehended only as knowledge itself. He who knows Brahman becomes Brahman!

4.24 "Sat-chit-ananda is everywhere. It's the original seed."

Jean Dunn, the disciple of Sri Nisargadatta Maharaj, said "Nothing can prevent the Self from realizing itself." The whole process of creation, with all its various beings in their diverse forms, is the expression of the power of the Self as it evolves towards Self-consciousness. The forms themselves, with their innate desire for positive experience, for pleasure, and for happiness, are all ultimately born because the Self wants to realize itself. They are all tending towards the fulfillment of that final desire that is inherent in the original seed, *sat-chit-ananda.*

In the human being, the Self becomes identified with the false sense of "I" or ego. There is then the belief that "I" am seeking happiness for "my" benefit. When you become a spiritual seeker, that illusion remains so that you imagine "I am an aspirant" and "I am seeking liberation." When, through the grace of the Master, Self-realization actually occurs, it is understood that there never was any such seeker. It was the Self all along that was drawing Itself to Itself in a purely imaginary game of separation. When this happens, the game is over, and the Self rests contented in Itself, as far as that individual body-mind is concerned. However, the game goes on in all the other myriad forms.

4.25 "In Oneness, there is neither joy nor sadness."

Sat-chit-ananda is actually intended to point to Oneness, even though it has three parts. *Ananda* is often translated as "bliss," which might imply that there is some kind of pleasurable experience in reality. A more traditional translation is "fullness," which better describes that which is complete in itself and which is beyond opposites such as joy and sorrow. It is clear that there has to be someone there to experience an emotion such as sorrow. Joy, as the opposite emotion to sorrow, is subject to the same limitation. In reality; that is, in Oneness, there is no individual person and therefore there can be no emotion, negative or positive.

4.26 "Animals, birds, even ants, all have the knowledge."

Even the tiniest creature is a manifestation of the same immortal Self. The Self is pure knowledge itself—it is always aware because it is itself absolute awareness. This knowledge is the *chit* aspect of the *sat-chit-ananda* triad, but *sat* (existence) and *ananda* (fullness) are always present as well. However, all creatures are also subject to the same illusion, which is the sense of individual existence caused by the identification of the Self with the form. Ironically, the higher up the evolutionary scale you go, the stronger this identification seems to be. A relatively simple form, such as a tree, may have little consciousness of its own existence, and may consequently enjoy relative peace and harmony. More complex forms, such as mammals, exhibit more and more restlessness and anxiety as a counterpart to their ability to experience affection and to think in a basic way. Human beings experience the greatest extremes of happiness and sadness of all creatures, because of their highly advanced capacity to conceptualize their own existence in relation to others. Nevertheless, individual existence remains false in the beginning, in the middle, and in the end, when it is finally seen as illusory.

4.27 "In effect, ignorance is the source of consciousness or knowledge."

Unlike animals, birds, insects, etc., a human being is capable of knowing its true nature. That is what makes it the greatest and highest of all creatures. Ignorance of that true nature is pervasive in all creatures—and in non-human forms there is no possibility of that ignorance going away—but through a human birth, the Self may realize itself as the One reality. If it were not for ignorance, everyone would live consciously as the Self. As it is, though, the Self identifies itself with whatever form it has manifested and, in this ignorance, the sense of individual existence, or individual consciousness, arises.

It may take a long time of bouncing to and fro in this state of individual consciousness, swinging wildly between the opposites of pleasure and pain, joy and suffering, before the Self manifests itself in the form of a human being who lives with the definite goal of finding the Self. At this point, the Self is seeking itself in the form of a seeker. Ignorance remains in the form of the concept "I am seeking the Self." However, this is the final stage before the Self brings the game to an end.

4.28 "Ignorance is in thinking you are the doer."

There is no "you" and no "doer." To think that you exist as the doer is ego. That is one definition of the ego. The actual nature of the ignorance is very hard to define. It is a state of "not-knowing" that persists throughout the life, appearing the same way every morning with the waking state. You cannot really see or understand this state of ignorance from within it. To think about the Self or God in ignorance is like having a thought about waking up in the middle of a dream. It remains only a thought and does not have any effect. You may think that you should do this or that in order to awaken, but you are only murmuring in your sleep. On the other hand, to think about waking up in the dream does happen and is right and appropriate. Awakening follows at the proper time.

4.29 "The power, which is so subtle, which makes everything work, can you feel it? Why? Because it is nothing."

The divine power that creates the world and makes everything happen is the power of *Maya*, illusion. *Maya* is the power of *Brahman*. To experience His power, *Brahman* has manifested himself as the world. If you are the sun, do you feel your own heat and see your own light? They are the effects of your existence, not your existence itself. The light of the sun is visible to the one who looks at it, not to the sun. The tremendous power of a flowing river is reduced to nothing at its source. A shadow is nothing to the one who casts it.

4.30 "Knowledge is the greatest ignorance."

Out of ignorance, knowledge has emerged. The thought comes "I am a person." The Self has identified Itself with the form and the name. The game goes on in this way, life after life, as long as ignorance remains. Happiness remains elusive, appearing tantalizingly for a short while, then receding again, leaving only a nagging desire for more. Desires are pursued, ends gained, something is won and something is lost. Death silences the person, which disappears as mysteriously as it appeared. Another person appears, lives a little time, and then also vanishes. This is the nature of knowledge. To take it to be true is the greatest ignorance.

5

May: The "Problem" of the Ego

5.1 "I was never born."

If you have a problem, you need to find a solution. If you don't have a problem, then there is no need to find a solution. So Maharaj taught that you should first of all find out if there is really a problem. There may be a feeling of dissatisfaction and you can say that that is the problem, but the question is whether that dissatisfaction is there because of something fundamentally lacking in you. It may be that there is nothing fundamentally wrong and that the dissatisfaction is caused by some wrong concept that you have about yourself. If that is the case, then the problem is not real, it is only an apparent problem that will go away as soon as you let go of the false concept.

We do have a false concept of ourselves. That false concept consists in the belief that we were born as individual entities and must therefore die. The one who was born is the one who has the problem of death. But where is the evidence that what you actually are was ever born? How can you know for sure as long as you don't know who or what you really are? To be free of the fear of death, you must know beyond any doubt that you were never born.

5.2 "Don't think 'I am doing these things to acquire reality.' You are He."

You can create a problem for yourself if you try too hard, or if you try in the wrong way. There is actually nothing to acquire because you are already the Self. My own experience was that at a certain point in my search, it occurred to me that all the efforts I was making to "remember myself," "be here now," and to be detached from life's circumstances were all being done because I felt that "I" had something to gain. There was a rather sudden understanding that it was in fact the ego that was trying to acquire reality and also trying to eliminate itself!

When this happened, I entered a phase in which I felt that I couldn't do anything. I abandoned my ego-centric efforts but I felt helpless. I drifted along like this for several years. Then I met Maharaj and he told me that I am already the reality, but I had not yet been able to accept it. That was the turning point for me, because, deep down, I already knew and felt that there is nothing to be gained. It was only a question of recognition of what was already the case. After that, understanding came very quickly.

5.3 "Examine the mind. 'Why you doubt?'"

Doubts are the manifestation of ignorance. They arise in the mind and occupy the place that should be reserved for the simple acceptance of reality. Why does the mind doubt? Is it anything but habit? That habit may go back a long way—it may be based on *sanskaras* from many lives—but it is still only a habit and, as Maharaj said, habits can be changed. Faith in the Master, and the grace that comes with it, are stronger than any habit.

5.4 "Mind always thinks of what doesn't exist."

Can the mind think of what really does exist? Since the very beginning, the saints and sages have stated very clearly that reality, the One Self that really exists, cannot be conceived in any way. The mind simply cannot reach it. What does that leave for the mind to think about?

Only the fleeting and insubstantial forms that are here today and gone tomorrow.

5.5 "Forget 'I' and He is there."

As soon as the sense of being an individual "doer" is released, there is peace and relaxation. Actually, this happens fairly frequently in ordinary life; for example, when you sit down to rest after completing some task, but it may not be recognized for what it is. To recognize your true nature as it already exists is really the point. Sri Ramana Maharshi said that there is no one who is not Self-realized, all that is necessary is to get rid of the thought that you are not realized.

Who is going to forget "I?" Can the "I" forget itself? The ego is not going to commit suicide. Fortunately, it isn't necessary to get involved in that kind of pointless struggle. The ego is really only a thought, or, to put it another way, a habitual way of thinking, that makes you believe, and then actually feel, that you are in bondage. If you hold on to the positive thought "I am He" that will help to weaken the ego in the early stages, but the final solution really only becomes possible when you understand that nothing can be accomplished through the mind. Then you place your head at the Master's feet, surrender yourself completely, and pray for his grace.

5.6 "Bondage and liberation are in the mind."

The aspirant comes to the Master and says "Master, I have become a cat." The Master replies "No, you are a human being, not a cat." The aspirant then of course says "In that case, how did I become a cat?" What can the Master say? There is no cat.

This is the situation with bondage and liberation. The problem is not real, only apparent. There isn't really a correct answer to the question "How to get liberation?" because the question itself is not valid, being based on a false assumption. However, the Master will typically make allowances for the fact that the aspirant has the conviction of bondage and will say something like "It has happened because of ignorance."

5.7 "I do not exist. I am not."

The whole of human interaction and human society is based on the assumption that there are separate individuals everywhere, each of whom is responsible for his or her own actions. Western-style society, law, and economic organization would be impossible without this fundamental premise. Only a very few realize the truth that no such individual persons ever existed in reality and that the notion of individuality itself is nothing more than a convention. If this truth ever became widely known and accepted, human society could hardly exist in its current form.

"I" is misunderstood and misinterpreted. The ordinary conception of "I," referring to an individual personality, is so far from the truth that it becomes almost absurd to speak about it. This "I" is purely conventional, a creation of the functioning of mind and memory. And yet the everyday world revolves around it and caters to its desires as though it had some real existence. A true teacher will explain that the real meaning of "I" is infinite consciousness, and that any other understanding is false.

5.8 "It is only in the mind that I've done good or bad."

Maharaj said that there are two ways to approach reality: one is to say "I don't exist, only He exists," and the other is to say "I am He, everything is myself." These two roughly correspond to the traditional paths of *bhakti* (devotion) and *jnana* (knowledge). On neither of these two paths is there any possibility of anyone actually performing any good or bad actions. If "I" do not exist, then the actions are not mine. If "I" am He, then the actions are His. You are already living in perfect freedom from the consequences of good and bad actions, but the ego-mind lays claim to them, assumes responsibility, and so perpetuates itself, going round and round in the circle of ignorance.

5.9 "'I' is only a thought."

I remember once in the Gemini Hotel on my first visit to Bombay, waking up in the middle of the night, jumping out of bed, and pacing up and down, the thought repeating over and over: "Everything is thought, including yourself!" That sudden understanding had occurred in sleep and was sufficiently powerful to grab the mind and shake it awake. The thought of my own existence was nothing but that; a single thought. It was just a concept that had appeared and would, in due time, disappear. Where would I be then? That was the question that shook me.

5.10 "Ego is knowledge, ego is mind, and mind is nothing but thought."

The word "mind" is convenient but does it really signify anything in itself? Surely there is no mind apart from the thought that is arising at any moment; the mind is nothing apart from its content. The thought of "I" is the ego. This "I" thought is the fundamental, basic thought, to which many other thoughts become attached. It returns persistently every morning because there is a pervasive belief in its reality. Its central role is taken for granted. It is the essential concept on which the mind rests, and it is, to all intents and purposes, synonymous with mind. Ego, the I-thought that is the basis of the mind, is itself knowledge, the knowledge of my own existence, "I am." That single thought underlies all other thoughts and takes the place of the true sense of "I," which is impersonal, universal.

5.11 "The power doesn't do anything. The ego says 'I did it.'"

Sitting quietly, doing nothing,
Spring comes and the grass grows by itself.

This Chinese verse shows how the power works, without effort, without volition. The concept that there is someone here who is the doer of the actions is really just a mistake, a misunderstanding. Imagine how beautiful it would be to live with absolutely no effort. That is perfect freedom. Not wanting to change anything, not expecting or desiring more or less than what actually is. In this vision, the ego is simply unnecessary.

5.12 "Say to the ego 'You are in my service. I am not in yours.'"

There is an old analogy that is found in the *Katha Upanishad* about the horse, the chariot, the passenger, and the driver. The driver, which is the mind, or ego, controls the horse, which represents the senses of the body. However, the real control is with the passenger, who is the "I." If the person is realized, the I just sits back and enjoys the ride with no worries. In those who never make any attempt to understand their own nature, the passenger is asleep, the driver is drunk, and the horse pulls the chariot this way and that. The ego-mind must sober up, become a good servant, and start listening to the quiet voice of the "I" within before a person can even start to understand a spiritual teaching.

5.13 "Mind fears and that is its support. Take out that support."

The root of fear is the feeling of separation that comes from consciousness taking itself to be a distinct individual. The mind fears many things and is full of big and small anxieties. One of the things it fears most of all is the disapproval of other people. "What will they think of me?" Or it may be a fear of not being able to manage, not having enough money to pay the rent. Whatever it is, the effect of fear in the mind is to support its sense of separation. Fear justifies keeping the thoughts focused on the external, on worldly affairs. The thoughts keep arising "I must do this. I must do that."

If you have a serious illness or you have no proper means of livelihood, of course these things should be taken care of. My own experience was that I had to have a steady job with low stress, a secure place to live, and a relatively harmonious marriage relationship before I could focus properly on Maharaj's teaching.

Once these basic needs have been met, it should then be possible to replace the mind's tendency to fear with trust in the Master. Trust in the Master is also trust in oneself and it includes an unspoken understanding that you will always be taken care of. I have verified time after time, so that I can no longer have the slightest doubt, that reality is absolutely trustworthy.

5.14 "I take bondage on myself."

You could perhaps sum up the main point of this teaching like this: "Before seeking liberation, find out if you are bound." You are already free, so the only problem is the thought "I am bound." Liberation, Self-realization, doesn't give you anything you don't already have. It only removes that wrong assumption of bondage. So this way can be very fast, if you can just grasp this main point.

5.15 "Submerge your ego. Do not be afraid of it."

There is a saying in the *I Ching* (Hexagram 43, *Breakthrough*) that goes like this:

The best way to fight evil is to make energetic progress in the good.

This seems to me to be an excellent motto for dealing with the ego, which represents all that is evil in oneself. Sometimes people will think of the ego as a powerful force that fights for its survival and is always cooking up some scheme to deceive them. I have never found this a useful approach. It is basically an admission of fear and lack of trust and it gives power to the ego. I have always found it better to focus on the positive and to continue to work on understanding the Master's teaching and surrendering to him. If you do that, then the ego will get weaker and weaker like a muscle that is not exercised. You really don't need to pay much attention to it. The most important thing to remember about the ego is that it is essentially only a thought. If you don't think that thought, then where is the "problem" of the ego?

5.16 "If the ego blocks your path, crush it. Let others make their comments."

Maharaj frequently encouraged us to become aware of our own power, which is absolutely capable of crushing the ego or brushing it aside like a fly. From time to time, as you progress, it may become necessary to react to obstacles in yourself in an extreme way. For example, you might find it necessary to leave the place you are living in or leave a relationship with someone who is not supporting you. The ego will resist change of its habitual patterns and so you may need to do some crushing! If you just act in accordance with your highest understanding at these critical points of your life you will do fine. When you have to act, you will be given the strength to do so, and you won't worry about what others think.

5.17 "Duality makes 'I'."

Consider the analogy of the sun and its rays. If you are yourself the sun, you are not aware of any rays, or of any of the other characteristics that humans attribute to the sun, such as intense heat, fire, and so on. In fact, you are not aware of anything at all. Now imagine someone holding up a mirror in front of you. Now you are aware of your own light rays and your heat. By becoming aware of these qualities, you become aware of yourself; in fact, you experience yourself *as* those qualities. You essentially become your own object.

This is exactly how it is with "I." Reality is "I without 'I';" that is, pure being without any experience of "I" or "I am." When you are in a state of deep sleep, you are in that non-dual condition. You are not aware of anything; there is no "I" until duality comes when you wake up in the morning. Then you say "I had a good rest."

5.18 "Mind does not want to die, so it goes toward wordly objects."

Preoccupation with wordly affairs is the mechanical activity of the mind. For many lives, it occupies itself with day-to-day concerns right up until the moment that the body breathes its last breath. Sri Nisargadatta Maharaj told a story about the man who, on his death-bed, noticed out of the window the family cow in the shed next door chewing the end of the best broomstick. He cried out "the broomstick, the broomstick!" and those were his last words.

The mind doesn't want to die in the sense that it has the built-in urge to continue as the doer, to perpetuate itself as the one who acts. In the long run, however, it is a mechanism that is bound to fail. Eventually, the search for meaning and happiness starts to turn inwards. The mind continues to live on, all through the spiritual search, until Self-knowledge dawns. It then continues to function, but is effectively dead as a center of volition. There is no need for that artificial center because the "I" of the realized person is always in harmony with the divine power.

5.19 "Death of the mind or ego is what is required."

There can easily be misunderstanding about what "death of the mind" means. There is no sudden blankness when the ego dies, although there is the ending of ignorance. After realization, the mind is still there and thoughts continue to appear and disappear, but there is no longer the illusion that "I am the doer." The ego sustained itself through the assumption that it was the center of the individual person. It had duties, desires, good and bad thoughts and feelings. All these things accrued to its account. The so-called "liberation" is the destruction of this account. The ego is then no longer active as a center of volition. Its power was a derived power that came from unquestioning belief in it. When ignorance goes, the ego cannot and does not survive.

5.20 "Ego means I am, and I know everything."

The ego is an artificial center for the experiencing of imaginary emotions, many of which are negative, such as judgment of oneself and others, irritation, anxiety, and so on. It is the embodiment of ignorance and the focus for wrong thinking of every kind. To take oneself to be a body, ruled by an individual ego is a very sad state of affairs. In the *Mundaka Upanishad* it says:

Fools, dwelling in darkness but wise in their own conceit and puffed up with vain scholarship wander about, being afflicted by many ills, like blind men led by the blind.

Because the ego is unreal, it has to maintain its apparent existence by gaining knowledge of worldly things. It continues to collect more and more knowledge on various subjects because this provides stimulus and creates some sensation of meaning in the mind. You only have to look at the list of titles from any university publishing house to see the kind of topics that the most highly educated people in our society find worthy of serious study. Of what use is all that knowledge if you do not know yourself?

5.21 "The ego is nothing. It has no entity at all."

There is an amusing and instructive story at the beginning of Chapter 2 of Sri Siddharameshwar's book *"Master Key to Self Realization"* about Gomaji Ganesh and his stamp. The story goes that in a certain town, no court of law could accept a document if it did not bear the stamp of "Gomaji Ganesh, the Brass Door." This went on for many years until finally, someone asked in court why a document that is valid in all other respects should be refused because it does not have, in addition, this particular stamp. Enquiries were then made and it turned out that Gomaji Ganesh was an insignificant functionary who had taken advantage of some moment of power to require that his stamp be added to all official documents. Siddharameshwar then points out:

It is not necessary to describe how the stamp was looked on with ridicule since that day when this decision was taken by the Court.

I really enjoy this story because it shows how it is the unquestioning assumption of its validity that gives power to the ego. The story also emphasizes how quickly that power can be taken away from it through a simple process of enquiry.

5.22 "Desire is will. When desire is for reality, ego goes off."

For all our protestations that we are creatures of free will, we are actually following whatever desire is the strongest. If there is a desire for something, and it is not offset by a stronger desire, we will generally try and fulfill it. In mathematical terms, will is a resultant of the vectors of the various desires, which are going in different directions.

Desire for reality is sometimes called the final desire or the desire that ends all other desires. It is the one-pointed aspiration for truth. It cannot be said to come from the ego, because in the pursuit of that desire, the ego itself will die. As the mind becomes increasingly turned towards the Self, it finds itself less and interested in mundane matters and may completely lose interest even in the things in which it took the greatest pleasure. These are all signs that the ego is growing weaker.

5.23 "Let your ego go to hell."

You cannot expect the ego to kill itself off. The ego has to go by a process of substitution, which is done by the guru, that is, it is done by accepting the Master's teaching. If you become properly engaged in that process, the ego will certainly go to hell. When your mind is focused on the final desire for reality, there is less and less room for the ego. Finally, the I-thought resolves itself into its source and the ego has nowhere to go.

5.24 "Unless you leave the body-mind, you can't be He."

The important question is always "Where is my sense of self, my sense of identity?" Am I identified with the concerns of the body-mind or am I thinking only of the eternal Self? Leaving the body-mind does not mean renouncing everyday life for the sake of sitting and meditating somewhere, but to turn away from the wordly life internally. Wherever the heart goes, the thoughts will follow.

5.25 "Forget the ego and you won't ever feel any sadness."

Sometimes someone will ask "What is the purpose of Self-realization?" This question is rather like asking "What is the purpose of happiness?" Self-realization means the end of all sadness because it involves the death of the ego, which is the source of sadness. You rediscover the source of happiness as your own being, right now. The ego, with its expectations and demands, its complaints and criticism, was distracting your attention from the fact that you were already free from sadness and sorrow.

5.26 "The ego is such a dirty, nonsense thing. It makes all the trouble and confusion in the world."

What is the ego, that it can be the cause of so much trouble? One definition is that it is the strong conviction that you are a separate individual. If you think that you are separate in a world of separate individuals, you create for yourself a world of competition, not cooperation, and your strongest instinct is to preserve and protect what you consider to be your own interests and the interests of those whom you identify yourself with. If you look at human society, from the level of the family up to the level of nations, you will see that it is organized on that basis.

It is not a bad thing to love yourself, if you love yourself in the right way, but loving yourself as opposed to others will produce bad results because it is exclusive and divisive, and that is a denial of the way things are in reality. Self-love that arises naturally from the recognition of your true nature as universal consciousness is a very positive force for good because that love is love that is without any object. Therefore it includes everything. In fact when we love anyone or anything, it is really the Self that is loving and the Self that is being loved. In the *Brihandaranyaka Upanishad*, it says:

It is not for the sake of itself, my beloved, that anything whatever is esteemed, but for the sake of the Self.

5.27 "Mind will never allow you to go to the reality because its death is there."

Maharaj equates mind with ego, and ego with knowledge. All three are the same, all pointing to the sense of your own existence as "I," which is the cause of all the trouble. Mind or ego will not allow you to go to the reality. It never can go to the reality, because reality has no sense of "I." It is a very simple equation: reality equals no "I," "I" equals no reality. However, even though the mind will never go to reality, there is absolutely nothing that can prevent reality from realizing itself when the time comes. If you cannot find God, then God will have to find you. This is in fact what is happening throughout the spiritual search and which becomes clear when that search comes to an end.

5.28 "The ego will never leave you. You will have to leave it."

Here is part of a fine poem by Swami Nirbhayananda, who lived in North India in the nineteenth century. It describes the separation from the ego-mind:

Your thoughts are restless, mine are forever peaceful.
You are attached to name and form.
I transcend them.
O dear one, I will have no more to do with you.

O mind, part company with me:
I salute you a thousand times.
You are all pain and tears,
I am peace and perfection.

The ego will never leave you because it *is* that "you" that thinks and talks and asserts itself as a person. How then, can "you" part company with it? The only way this is possible is through the understanding that the "you" that you took yourself to be is not you and that "you" do not exist at all in that sense of being a separate person. Then you remain always, not as an individual, but as the reality that is in everything.

5.29 "The ego is always looking for some benefit for itself; I must be respected, loved, or recognized."

There are literally thousands of books that deal with the psychology of the ego; how it became so fundamentally insecure, and how to make it less so. On the way of Self-enquiry, we don't take any notice of these kind of methods, because they are all based on the false assumption that the ego-mind is oneself. Of course, as long as you believe that that is the case, you have to take the mind seriously and, if it seems to be broken, you have to try and fix it.

The ego is a mechanism with a limited number of reactions, like a tape that always plays the same few songs over and over. It has become the center for all kinds of demands and expectations and, left to itself, it will pursue those wants and demands to the body's last breath. The whole process of its appearance and growth through the course of a lifetime has been a process of creating nothing from nothing. Out of nothing comes the concept "I am somebody," and that concept collects other concepts "I want love, respect, recognition." It has no meaning, no purpose. It is a virtual machine, functioning in the only way it can. What is amazing is that into all this mechanical functioning the thought "Who am I, really?" finally appears and from that spring, the water of understanding begins to flow. In its own time, the spring becomes a flood that submerges the thought of the separate ego.

5.30 "Rama himself became Ravanna. Ravanna doesn't exist so how can he kill him?"

In the epic myth of the Ramayana, the demon-king Ravanna represents the ego. He is illusive and hard to kill because he is actually an aspect of Rama, the Self. Everything is the Self. There is no second thing, and so Rama becomes Ravanna when his true nature is concealed from himself by ignorance. As long as Rama splits himself into two and identifies himself with Ravanna, he cannot kill him. He cuts off one of the demon's heads and another one springs up to replace it! Rama first has to understand that reality is one and that he is that one. Then the arrow flies to Ravanna's heart and kills him. The sense of "I" returns to the Self, where it belongs, and, like a piece of salt falling into the ocean, the individual consciousness merges with the universal consciousness.

5.31 "The ego is like the barren woman's son. It doesn't exist, but still you say 'I've done it.'"

In the end, the ego has one fundamental weakness, one flaw which it can never overcome, which is that it doesn't exist! The "problem" of the ego is an apparent problem, not a real one. The sense of separation that is the principal effect of belief in the ego can go away in a moment, if the reality of the Self is fully known. Your natural state is happiness, free from any sense of separation, free from wanting and dissatisfaction, free from ignorance and doubt. How fortunate is the aspirant, who, at the end of a long search, finds the true guru, the one who shows what real freedom is and who provides the means to realize it!

6

June: Being an Aspirant

6.1 "You must ask questions until you fully understand."

Being an aspirant means being someone who has questions. It is a process of living the questions until you grow into the answer. Then you live the answer and have no questions anymore. Until that full or final understanding comes, finding the answer to questions is the way of life for an aspirant. A sincere seeker will always be successful. The guru, or Master, will provide the answer to all the aspirant's questions, either by answering verbally during *satsang* or non-verbally by providing understanding directly in response to a prayer or inner request. This second option is possible because the true guru is within you. It is never a problem to receive an answer to a sincere question, even after the physical body of the Master is no longer available. The most important thing you can do is to formulate the right questions and keep them in your mind—"live them"—until the answer comes in the form of understanding.

6.2 "What you've got, be satisfied with that."

As long as you are an aspirant, you cannot and should not be satisfied with anything less than final understanding. So this statement does not refer to understanding but only to the external circumstances of life. If you are not satisfied with your situation in life, it is inevitable that you will invest a lot of time and energy in making it more to your liking. The question is: "Why am I doing that?" Is the goal to arrange my life so that I am free from distractions and can devote myself to worship and study, or am I doing it because I am attached to having a better house, a better relationship, and so on, for their own sake?

If you can be satisfied with little in the way of possessions and have few desires, that is very helpful. Time and energy is limited in this life. If you have ten grammes of gold, you can have it beaten into gold leaf and can gild one object with it, but you can't gild four or five objects. Here is a verse by Farid, a Punjabi poet who lived in the thirteenth century:

Be contented with your lot
Don't envy what others have.
Tie a wooden loaf to your belly.
Eat what is doled out to you.
Don't cast longing glances at delicacies others eat.
Relish the cold water and plain food
That fall to your share.

6.3 "Be in the water, but don't take the touch of it."

The lotus leaf rests on the surface of the water, floating peacefully, but it does not get wet, that is, it does not absorb the water. If it did, it would sink. This is an example of how to live, free from the emotional disturbance that comes from identifying with the objects of the world. When there is a desire, you may just let it pass like water flowing off the leaf, or you may allow that desire to enter. Then you say "I want" or "I must have," and, taking that desire as yourself, you find no peace until you fulfill it. You must then accept the fruits of the brand new *karma* that has been created. In this way, the wheel of life, death, and rebirth continues to turn.

6.4 "What I understand up to now is all wrong."

As long as you imagine that you know something about reality, you are bound by ignorance. Many people have partial knowledge gained from reading. When they meet a real Master, they compare what he says with what they feel they already know and so find it impossible to accept what the Master says. This happens all the time. Things are not arranged so that everyone can accept what the Master says. The purpose of the Master's teaching is to show you that your concepts about yourself are all wrong. At some point, you have to agree with that proposition and be willing to let go whatever it is that you believe you understand about who you are. Then the mind becomes free for the process of Self-enquiry that leads to Self-knowledge.

6.5 "Let the world go to Heaven or Hell, I don't care. Be this determined."

The Way of the Bird (*vihangam marg*) is really the way of Self-enquiry (*vichara marg*). The goal is to understand "Who am I?" In the process of discovering who you are, you necessarily lose interest in external objects. This detachment or turning away from the world is traditionally called *vairagya*. Attention turns inwards, in the direction of the source of consciousness itself. One of the ironies of the spiritual search is that you have to deny reality to the whole world of objects, only to find out later that the world is not other than yourself. However, during the process of Self-enquiry, it is right and appropriate to develop a one-pointed focus, a determination to find the source of the "I." Then you will say "Let the world go to Heaven or Hell. Let it be whatever it is, I am concerned only to know reality."

6.6 "You have to practice "I'm not the body, not the knowledge, not the ego."

The human birth is a wish-fulfilling tree (*kalpataru*). It gives whatever you request of it. It is only because you bring to it the thoughts "I am a small separate creature" and "I want only small, insignificant, worldly things" that you remain stuck in the circle of ignorance. As soon as you shift your desires to something bigger and your aspirations to something higher, you immediately start to get results.

You may say "I want only reality," but you cannot know what reality is. You can only know what is not reality. Therefore, the process of Self-enquiry is essentially a process of elimination. This is why Maharaj says to practice in this way, by dis-identifying with the body, the knowledge, and the ego.

6.7 "Your habits must be changed, so practice is necessary, otherwise it's impossible."

Practice (*sadhana*) is needed as long as you are an aspirant. One definition of "aspirant" is someone who practices for the purpose of discovering the truth about his or her own nature. Changing habits is not an end in itself. Changing the habits of the mind is a part of the means, part of the method. We are born in ignorance of our true nature and we adopt wrong ideas of who we are along with the development of the mind itself. This habit of wrong thinking must be changed. This is not psychotherapy, which attempts to make the mind function more harmoniously in a world that is itself the product of the mind. On this way, the practice is to find the root or the source of the I-thought; "What does "I" really refer to?" As a result of this practice, you will also discover what the world is.

6.8 "Always be negative (not this, not that)."

The Self is absolute reality. It cannot ever not exist. That Self has to be rediscovered as your own existence, as your own beloved, because nothing is dearer to you than your own Self. If it were possible to say exactly what the Self is, the great Masters and sages of the past would already have done so. Everything that can be said as a pointer towards the Self has already been said hundreds and thousands of times. Still the Self remains a puzzle that you have to solve for yourself. The sages of India therefore used the method of pointing out what is not the Self (*neti, neti*). You are not the body, not the mind, not knowledge. Anything and everything that can be perceived or conceived is to be recognized as not-Self, so that in the end the Self can be recognized as That which remains when all else is laid aside.

6.9 "Be attached to the reality and then you become real."

Maharaj often said that the mind is the only factor. You are reality already, so it is only a question of understanding that one thing. The whole business of spiritual practice is really about changing the way the mind looks at things. It is as though there is a mismatch between the fact and the perception of it, like looking at one of those optical illusions which show two patterns, but you can only see one of them at a time. Once you see the "other" pattern though, you can't understand how you didn't see it before. Being in ignorance about your true nature is to be stuck in a similar kind of thought pattern. That pattern doesn't correspond to reality, but you have become so accustomed to it that you take it to be the real thing.

So what does Maharaj mean here when he says "Be attached to the reality?" It is a question of turning the mind in the right direction and keeping it focused there. Sri Nisargadatta Maharaj said that in order to find something you have lost, you have to keep it in mind at all times until you find it again. This is good advice because the problem is not that what was lost is somewhere outside you. You know it is inside you. So you just need to keep your focus on reality. Then, more and more, you get the feeling that you can't be satisfied with anything other than final and complete understanding. You start to feel like the bath water spinning faster and faster as it goes down the drain. The less there is of me, the ego, the faster the understanding comes. Kabir puts it rather more poetically:

Saying "You, You" I became you
And shed this I-ness of mine.
Now wherever my eyes turn
I see only you.

6.10 "Don't be chicken-hearted. Have a Master's heart."

One thing about Maharaj was that he was always so encouraging! He wanted us all to adopt what they call in the USA a "can-do" attitude. Certainly, it is true that, in the final analysis, no-one does anything because there is no doer. However, this does not make for a useful attitude most of the time that one is an aspirant. It is much better to have this kind of "I am a true disciple of my Master and I can do anything (through his grace)" attitude. If you have problems, confront them, if the ego distracts you, crush it, if people don't support you, let them go to Hell!

6.11 "Die yourself. You should die. "I am not this."

Death of course is a very frightening proposition as long as you take yourself to be the body-mind. To remove that fear, you have to arrive at the conviction that what you are in reality is not anything that could ever be born or die. That conviction or realization actually means the "death" of the ego, which is the only thing that is ever born, in this life or in any other. Here is a verse from the saint Dadu Dayal, who lived in the sixteenth century:

Hurrah! My foe I is dead
No one can now kick at me.
I've destroyed myself
And thus dying I live on.

6.12 "Do not say that only realized beings are great. You, yourself, is great."

Any one of us can be raised to the level of the Master. The Master is God and his grace is always ready to make a Master out of the disciple. It is not that he waits for a disciple who is completely pure and spotless. He might have to wait for an eternity! Rather he waits for the disciple who sincerely wants reality and who asks for it as his or her only desire. When the Master finds a disciple like this, he reaches down and pulls the devotee up to his own level of greatness.

The true devotee never doubts that it is possible for him or her to become a Master. In fact, that is taken to be the whole purpose of the Master's teaching. Maharaj would not have bothered teaching at all had he not known that it was perfectly possible for his disciples to become what he was. He knew, because that is what happened to him with his own Master. One of the obstacles that some disciples face is that they do not believe that it is possible for them to attain the level of the Master; they feel he is too great, so they prefer to worship the guru as though he were a God, a being who remains high above them. This attitude is completely contrary to what the Master teaches and to what he wants for his disciples.

6.13 "Forget all the wishes of your body-mind."

What does the body-mind typically wish for? Food, drink, sexual experience, new possessions of various kinds, entertainment, novelty, and physical and mental stimulation through travel, reading, listening to various teachers, and so on. Is it really necessary to forget all of these things for Self-knowledge to come? This is rather like asking "Is it necessary for all the leaves to fall off the tree for Winter to come?" Just as the leaves fall off as Winter approaches, so the desires of the body-mind fall away as desire for the Self fills your thoughts. How many of the desires listed above does a realized person have? How many leaves are left on the tree in Midwinter?

6.14 "When wish is for reality, it is not called ego."

The wish for reality, or desire for liberation, is the most important qualification of the aspirant. In traditional *Vendanta* teaching, it is called *mumukshutva*. The reason it is so important is that it is this desire for reality that transforms itself into Self-knowledge. Through seeking reality, you finally come to the surprising realization that you, the one who was seeking, are yourself the reality. Then you understand that this wish for reality is actually reality drawing itself to itself, as though the ocean was commanding all the rivers of the world to flow into it and become one with it. The wish for reality is itself the grace of the Master.

6.15 "Don't feel sorrow or anything. Be brave enough to accept whatever happens."

In the West, we are conditioned to feel sorrow in all sorts of situations, in particular when someone dies. But does the dead person feel sorry? Sorry is considered appropriate because we are supposed to hold onto the concept that the individual person is precious and that this life is the only one that the soul goes through. In India, on the other hand, death is not such an occasion for weeping and wailing, because it is taken for granted that there will be another life, and that what is not accomplished now will be accomplished later. Consequently, there is less fear and anxiety attached to the thought of dying.

God, the Master and Lord of all, is the only power that is operating in the Universe. The only thing that matters with regard to the events that happen in life is whether you accept them as His will or not. If you cannot accept something that happens, you suffer unnecessarily. Such resistance is typical of the ego, which always thinks of itself as the doer. "How can this happen to ME?" it says. When you have surrendered this imaginary will to the Master, however, you not only feel that what happens is His will, but you feel that it is *your* will as well. There isn't any difference. You have the feeling that what is happening is all right with you and you know that your needs will be taken care of. Saint Tukaram wrote:

Just like a cow always thinks of her calf, the Saints love me unconditionally and offer me refuge, protecting me everywhere.

6.16 "Do not let your enemy enter your home."

Ego is the enemy. If you try to use the ego to destroy the ego or try to use your mind to purify the mind, it is like asking the thief to pursue the thief. The thief will pretend to chase the thief but nothing will come of it. Therefore, it is better to set one's sights beyond the mind. The best practice is just to listen to the Master's teaching, and let it take over the mind. As long as you accept what he says and surrender to Him, the ego has no room to enter. Kabir wrote:

Narrow is the lane of love
God and I can't co-exist.
When I was, He wasn't there
Now He's there, I'm not.

6.17 "Be very strong in yourself. I tell you that you are the reality and that you can experience this."

The Master holds out an invitation to us. He gives us the address of the house of the Self and says "Go there and go inside. Take possession of what is yours." That is all he can do. He can't understand and accept for us. That strength we have to find for ourselves. Strength may not look like strength. In my own case, it was more a feeling that there was nothing else to care about. I felt that devotion to the Master was all that I had. I felt very helpless. So strength may feel like weakness. The strength that is needed is the power to discriminate between what you can do without and what you can't do without, what you are holding onto out of habit, and what it is that you really want. So Maharaj is making a very definite statement here that if you really want reality, you can have it. It's up to you now.

6.18 "When there is no faith, then doubt always arises in the mind."

The Sanskrit word used in Vedanta for faith in this context is *shraddha*. This word includes the concept of trust in the competence of the teacher together with personal devotion to him. This is the kind of faith that keeps doubts from arising. As long as you trust your guru, any doubt can be destroyed simply by asking a question. This process will work through sincere prayer even after the guru has left the body. Aspirants who lack this kind of faith generally have a major problem with doubt, especially if they have semi-faith in more than one guru, because what one teacher says will inevitably appear to contradict what the other one says. This leads to a perpetual state of uncertainty. Faith in the sense of *shraddha*, that is, faith that includes personal devotion to one's Master, is important because it is the best way to free oneself of lingering doubts.

6.19 "If doubts come in the mind, ask the Master. If you don't, then doubts will remain."

The Master is the Self. He is within you, in fact he is everywhere, and so there is never any distance between you and him. All that is necessary is the attitude of confidence that all doubts can be cleared by trust in the Master. You just have to formulate the question or express the doubt that has arisen and then wait in full faith for the answer to come. Once a doubt has been cleared in this way, there's no reason why it should come back.

6.20 "To die means to forget everything. When you are living, die in that way."

The *jnani* (realized person) transcends the illusory identification with the body while still in the body. Others have to wait for the body to die to realize that the identification is false. To transcend illusion is to understand that it is all a projection of the Self, which is the eternal reality. To see everything as not separate from the Self means to forget everything, that is, the illusory separateness of the objects of the world is forgotten, no longer seen. That is the death and the resurrection also.

6.21 "Say 'I don't exist.' There is the death."

It is always worth remembering, I think, that when Maharaj said "I don't exist," he generally meant "I don't exist, only He exists." The concept of "I" not existing does not leave a void. "He" always remains and you are He. So you are always there, only not as the individual person that you took yourself to be. This false ego has to be surrendered, sacrificed. In his commentary on the fifth afternoon bhajan, Maharaj says:

The ego which is nothing you offer Him! And He gives you reality!

6.22 "Nothing is required of you, and there is nothing to acquire."

The truth is really very simple, so simple that the mind passes over it, expecting something more complex and difficult to attain. The mind is always focused on the waking state, because it is the creator of the waking state, and so it naturally looks for reality there. However, the waking state is just one of the states that appear and disappear while the Self always remains. For this reason, the mind can never find the Self. Ultimately, the whole process of seeking the Self is seen to be an impossible exercise, a dream journey, because you cannot find what you already are. It is not a question of acquiring anything and nothing special is required to understand the reality of your own existence beyond the three states of waking, dreaming, and deep sleep. The following verse is from the Kashmiri saint Lalla Yogeshwari, who lived in the fourteenth century:

I Lalla went round and round the world
In frantic search of the omnipresent Lord.
Coming back from my adventures I found
Him sitting in my body, His own home.

6.23 "Check your mind and a habit will be made and you will be OK."

I think it is clear that you cannot understand very much if the mind is just allowed to wander all over the place and get up to all kinds of tricks like a monkey. An unchecked mind is attracted to one thing, and then forgets about it when it is attracted to something else, just like the monkey swinging in the trees holds onto one branch until it has a grip on the next one. Therefore, it is necessary to instill some discipline in the mind, so that good behavior becomes a habit. The mind must learn to turn inwards and to focus more and more on the Self that is its source.

There is a story about a man who had a cow that was always going into neighboring gardens to eat the green grass there. The man brought fresh green grass into the cow-barn to encourage the cow to stay there and not wander. As the cow got used to finding the fresh grass in the barn every day, it stopped going into the gardens to find its food. Eventually, it would not go out even if the barn door was left open. Similarly, the mind that accepts the correct ideas from the Master quietens down and becomes one-pointed.

6.24 "One should leave the room, otherwise He can't enter."

Knowledge of worldly things and knowledge of God are incompatible. Because this human birth is a wish-fulfilling tree (*kalpataru*), what you receive is really a question of what you ask for, of what is occupying your heart. The heart is the room that must be emptied before He can enter. Saint Tukaram wrote:

When you have dismissed
All expectations
When there's nothing left
That you call your own
Surely the Lord is calling on you.

6.25 "When you follow your mind, you lose yourself, and that is the greatest loss."

The Self is always present, closer to you than anything else, but it is not known. Therefore the scriptures and sages say that Self-knowledge is the goal. Self-knowledge comes through the mind but it is not *of* the mind. The Self can be known by a mind that has turned inwards and is actively looking for its source. It can never be found by a mind that is directed outwards, towards the things of the world. A mind that is turned outwards will constantly produce desire-thoughts like "I want to do this, I want to do that" or judgment-thoughts like "this person is good, that one is bad." If you follow these thoughts by taking them to be yourself, then you do suffer the greatest loss, and go in the opposite direction to the Self-knowledge that alone can free you.

6.26 "If you don't take the medicine, how the disease can go?"

If you go to someone to ask for advice, surely you should be prepared to take that advice when it is offered? Otherwise, what is the point? Similarly, if you go to the doctor, describe your symptoms, and then receive medicine, surely you don't then put the medicine in a drawer and forget about it? Nevertheless, despite the obvious logic of these examples, the ego is always ready to sit at the feet of a spiritual teacher, ask questions and receive answers, and then do the opposite of what is suggested. Or it will doubt the appropriateness of the answer, or find some other way to render it ineffective. All this vacillation keeps the veil of ignorance drawn over the Self.

6.27 "When a doubt comes upon you ('How can I be That?' for example), you lose your strength."

Steady determination is what is required. Matched with faith and trust in the guru, you have an unassailable combination, as attested by many saints and sages through the centuries. A good example is Sri Nisargadatta Maharaj. He said:

My guru told me I am the final reality. That was good enough for me. I believed him and ceased to take an interest in what was not me nor mine.

Doubts are like obstacles on the path. They have to be cleared away so that progress can continue. Sometimes a doubt is just the mind not grasping something that seems logically inconsistent to its current level of understanding, for example, "How can I, the limited individual, be the same as That, the unlimited reality underlying all things?," in which case it can be resolved by asking the Master. At other times the doubt might be deeper and more emotional in nature, for example, "How can I, a small creature, ever hope to be as great as That?." This kind of doubt amounts to doubt in oneself and is a much more serious obstacle.

Once you realize that this kind of attitude is hindering your progress, you are already half way to dealing with it, because it is out in the open, no longer hidden. You could then ask yourself "What is it that I really want?" "Do I fully accept what the Master has said?" "Do I believe that I can become a realized person in this lifetime?" "Do I need to ask for His grace?" By an honest self-examination, even deep-rooted doubts can be cleared.

6.28 "You are here to get out of this circle of ignorance."

Ignorance is a circle because it is created and sustained by the ego, which is itself a product of ignorance. We are essentially born into ignorance, because, even though as infants we are abiding in the Self, we have no knowledge of it. Then later, when the ego develops into a full-fledged personality, we still have no knowledge of it, plus it is obscured still further by the identification of the "I" with the gross body. So this is the circle we are in when, for some unknown reason, something in us suddenly starts asking "Who am I really?" and the search begins.

6.29 "Knowledge belongs to the ego. But gaining that knowledge is an important step you must go through."

To get out of the circle of ignorance, the first thing you need is knowledge, information passed in to you from one who is already living in freedom outside of the circle. You need to know that there is a way out and you need to know what you need to do to find that way out. Certainly, it is the ego that takes up these new ideas in the beginning, but only because it has no idea that in the end it will itself have to die. By the time it figures out that part, it is already too late.

6.30 "You simply must get rid of the illusion of doing, which is imprinted on your mind."

The ego is obsessed with the idea of doing something. In fact, one definition of the ego is that it is "the sense of doership." One thing that is very noticeable is that as you go on and draw closer to final understanding, the sense of your doing anything becomes weaker and weaker. The concept of doing is really just a habitual way of thinking. As you stop attributing doership to yourself, you feel freer. You begin to see that He is doing everything for you, and that all you need to do is accept that, so that things can unfold as they must. Then the activity of the ego ceases to trouble you as much and you begin to walk in light instead of in darkness.

7

July: The Work of the Master

7.1 "Don't ask blessings of the Master. Be He, that is his blessing.

Saint Tukaram says in one of his verses that the real *prasad* is acceptance of reality. Similarly, the real blessing that one receives from the Master is the knowledge that you are He, the Self. This knowledge is not ordinary knowledge, because it has the power to transform the mind that hears it. Just as camphor, when it is lit, flares up and burns for a while, then disappears completely, so the mind that accepts the Master's blessing becomes no-mind. In the process, the false concept of the ego is destroyed, the "I" resolves itself back into its source, and the oneness of the Self is realized.

7.2 "Never ask anything from the Master (the mother knows when the child needs milk)."

The mother takes care of the child's needs. It is a natural response. The child does not have to ask the mother "Will you feed me or won't you?" Feeding just happens; the child is ready to be fed and the mother feeds it. In the same way, when understanding, or even Self-realization, is due, it just happens, quite naturally. There is really no need to ask for anything because what is bound to happen, will certainly happen at the appropriate time. On the other hand, if something is not due to happen, it will not happen. Not even the Master can give you what you are not ready for. Not understanding this law, many people come to a Master and say "Please give me your grace" or "Give me your blessing so that I can get Self-realization."

7.3 "Be always on the way your Master shows you, and you will be one with him."

As long as you are trying to do what the Master says, you will experience a natural flow of "blessings" arising in yourself. You will find the answers to questions appearing in yourself, and you will feel more and more satisfaction. On the other hand, if you only say you accept what he says but don't practice it, you will not feel in harmony with him or with yourself. The human body and mind is a wish-fulfilling tree (*kalpataru*) and it makes things appear exactly the way you conceive of them. If you trust the Master and follow the way he shows you, you can become what he is. If you don't believe it's possible, it won't be.

7.4 "Don't take your Master as an ordinary person."

The Master is like a spotlessly clean, perfectly polished mirror. When you go and sit at his feet, you feel immense peace, and in the beginning you may think: "Such peace radiating from this person!" Actually there is no radiation, no movement. It is your own peace that you are experiencing; the peace of the Self. The Master is Self only, there is no "ordinary person" there to obscure the being, consciousness, and fullness of reality. You also are Self only and as long as you can forget your own "ordinary person" you experience that same being, consciousness, and fullness in his presence.

7.5 "Most important in the beginning is the notion that he is my Master and what he says is correct."

No one can say why one person will meet a Master and accept him or her while another will not. Some say it is due to good *karma* from previous lives, some say it is just good luck. I don't know, but I do know that it is no small thing to become a true "son of the guru" (*guruputra*). Once you have said "He is my Master," you may leave him at some point but he will never leave you.

The problem that brings you to the Master is a problem of ignorance. You don't know what the truth is or who you really are, but you have a lot of ideas that you have accumulated that make you believe you can find something. The first opportunity that you have when you meet the Master is to put aside all those confused ideas and accept that what he says is correct. This first step immediately makes things much simpler and you are freer than you were before.

7.6 "Have complete faith in the Master, and afterwards faith is not required."

Real faith in the Master is not a blind faith that accepts every word without personal experience. However, it does mean that you do not doubt it. You accept what he says as correct pending your own verification. For example, if the Master says "You are He," then you know that that must be the truth, even though you may not immediately feel that way in your everyday experience. You accept it as correct and then find out for yourself the truth of it. Everything has to be experienced within yourself. Then faith is no longer required, because you have understood each truth intimately for yourself.

7.7 "Keep the touch of what the teacher says. That you keep the touch of!"

Maharaj uses the analogy of the lotus leaf, which floats on the water, but doesn't absorb the water. Here, though, he is saying "keep the touch of what the teacher says." You always want to identify yourself with something, so why not identify yourself with the Master's teaching? If you let yourself be deeply touched by his ideas, they will become part of you. Say "I leave my thoughts at your feet. Your thoughts are my thoughts now."

7.8 "You've become the mind, so Master changes your mind."

There is no "you" in reality, but that thought is there and it has become a conviction. There is a pervasive belief in individual existence. You have become that, and so you have to live the life of the mind, with all its stresses and anxieties. The guru-disciple relationship is a rescue line that has been in place for thousands of years. It works if the teacher is genuine and if the disciple is ready and willing to surrender his or her mind so that it can be changed by the guru's teaching. The Master tells you the truth, and continues to tell you the truth in a hundred different ways. He doesn't magically change your mind with a glance or a touch. Such experiences may happen but they can only be temporary. Permanent change depends on the ability to accept and understand what the Master says.

7.9 "The Master gives some force to these thoughts, so you have to go and see him."

The disciple's aspiration comes alive in the presence of the Master. The Master's words resonate in the disciple's mind and give strength to his or her conviction that the teaching is correct. The disciple is aware that, without the Master, understanding would not be possible. It is a love-relationship. Those who fall into this love-relationship with the Master are the most fortunate of people. Jnaneshwar devotes the second chapter of the *Amritanubhav* to honoring his guru, Nivritti. There are many beautiful verses and images. Here is just one of them:

He has attained the great status of Guru
By possessing no status.

His wealth is his ability
To rid us of what does not exist.

7.10 "You have taken a body and that ego always goes against the teaching of the Master."

The poet, Sri Dadaji Maharaj, who lived in Aligarh, North India in the nineteenth century, wrote:

False is the love of woman,
Of wealth, of power,
But the love of the guru
Is true love.

You are here to find your guru,
And having found him and accepted him
To become one with him.
It is better to cease from breathing
Than to desert the guru.

The body-mind will always go towards worldly things. That is all it knows. The ego is the embodiment of the illusion of individuality. Love for the Master is a great power that can destroy the ego, right down to its roots. It allows you to accept the Master's teaching and understand it. Without that power, the ego will not go.

7.11 "Whether the Master is with you or not, the faith you have in him takes you to the right level and then you do the right thing."

"Doing the right thing" is not just a figure of speech. It is essential to do the right things and avoid doing the wrong things if you want to realize. You feel like doing the right things when you feel complete faith in the Master. Then you remember his example and you want to be like him in the sense that you want to value what he values. Your sense of right and wrong has to come from him. You temporarily give up your will to him for as long as it takes to realize your true nature. After that happens, you can trust yourself because there is no difference between you and him.

7.12 "Loudspeaker speaks. He doesn't care if people hear or not."

The ego doesn't like to hear statements like this one, because it prefers to imagine that the Master feels something special for it as an individual. Of course this is not possible. The Master does not recognize individuals. He does not show favoritism but speaks consistently at all times. His job is to speak the truth and to point out the way to those who ask. He knows that those who are ready to hear will hear, and that those who are ready to surrender will do so. Kabir wrote:

O Kabir, I am looking for a true listener,
Who, like the deer, hearing the horn of the hunter,
Surrenders himself completely to him.
The Guru loves all, but he who loves the Guru
And serves him day and night,
He will taste the water of conscious immortality.

7.13 "He, the Master, is not there at all."

Those of us who met Maharaj and who sat at his feet cherish our memories of him. Of course, those memories are not real; snapshots do not capture the real person. Whatever you think or feel about the Master is in you. This is true for any object in the world. You cannot know it as it is in itself, you only know your own experience. The substance of objects is knowledge; if there is no knowledge, there is no object. So when you look at Maharaj sitting there, what you are seeing is your own image of him. He is not there as an object. In fact, the effectiveness of the Master's presence in making you feel your own inner peace and joy depends on the fact that he is not there. The Master is transparent, like space, and simply mirrors back to you your own spaciousness.

7.14 "The only thing the Master does is to give its real value to the power that is within you, to which you pay no attention."

The Master is not in the business of making something out of nothing. He is not interested in giving you some practice so that you may eventually acquire something. He only points out to you what is already there. The guru is the dispeller of darkness. He tells you that you are the reality. You already are That; you only need to get rid of the false assumption that you are not realized. The power of the Self: being, consciousness, fullness (*sat-chit-ananda*) is your own nature. There is never a moment when you can say that you are not. This means that you already realize the Self. The problem is that you pay no attention to this fact. So the Master sets you straight on this point.

7.15 "You have to submit to the Master. Why to worry for the illusion?"

By surrendering my mind to my Guru
I had it polished,
And now it is transparent.

This verse from Kabir expresses the essential change that happens through the guru-disciple relationship. The mind is covered in ignorance like a mirror covered in dust. That ignorance must be removed. This happens when the disciple surrenders his or her mind to the Master, replacing all the old ideas and assumptions with the new understanding provided by the Master's teaching. When the mind understands the correct ideas, it becomes quiet and can reflect the Self clearly. It becomes transparent to reality. Then the Self is known effortlessly, because the Self is always shining steadily, just like the sun that will always readily show its reflection in any still and clear water.

7.16 "Master is a pointer only. He takes you up to the door and he's finished. He doesn't remain there."

If you read the questions and requests that people bring to saints and sages, you often find the assumption that the Master can give understanding or even Self-realization to the disciple. How is that possible? Even if the Master did have such powers, how could realization be sustained if the mind of the aspirant was not properly prepared? At best, it would be just a taste. The Master can tell you everything you need to know, giving you the correct address. He answers your questions to clear every doubt, taking you up to the door. Then he is finished. It is up to you to take the final step, to enter the house and take possession of it.

7.17 "The Master says the whole world is going this way, come with me to my side."

The Master holds out the invitation to live with him in peace and happiness always. The love that you have for the guru makes it easier to give up what you have to give up. You think of him and you feel "He would never lie to me." The world is a dream that lasts for a while and then is gone. It is a wheel of frustration and desire, a circle of ignorance. Is it really so hard to let go? Kabir wrote:

Giving up all expectation of gain from the world,
Be like one who has died,
Alive only in service of the Guru and the Yoga.
Then God will run after you, saying:
"Oh Kabir, wait, I come!"

7.18 "There is neither disciple nor Master in the final understanding."

Final understanding is understanding that there is nothing to understand. The world is a spontaneous appearance. The one who perceives it is included in it as a character in the dream. In reality, there is no Master, no disciple, no teaching, and no realization. That all happened in the dream. Final understanding means freedom from the cycle of birth and rebirth: the current dream continues for its allotted time, and then is over. There is a famous quatrain from the *Rubaiyat* of Omar Khayyam:

There was a door to which I found no key:
There was a veil past which I could not see:
Some little talk awhile of me and thee
There seemed—and then no more of thee and me.

7.19 "The Master knows he doesn't do anything. The power in him does these things."

Who is there to do anything? Maharaj always said "I don't exist!" He meant it quite literally. The person we saw when we looked at him was our concept only. There is a divine, impersonal power that shapes all of these dream-lives, making them appear the way they do. It does so on the basis of universal laws that give to all alike the results of past actions. The life of the Master, also, is simply a living out of the effects of past actions. The difference is that the Master knows that the power does everything, while the ignorant person continues to believe that he or she is the doer of those actions.

7.20 "You have got the respect for the Master by mind, and keep that respect always."

When you first meet your Master, you may feel a great sense of peace. You feel different and that makes you want to listen to what he has to say. Respect for the Master comes in the mind when you begin to understand for yourself that what he says is correct. It increases when he clears your doubts by answering your questions. Then it is up to you to keep that respect by continuing to accept and understand his teaching.

Nowadays, we have so much choice, so many teachers and books are available, that is very easy to treat a Master as just one among many others. Even a century ago, the kind of "guru-hopping" that goes on today in the West would have been impossible. Respect for the guru was natural when it was very hard to find one. In the end, the aspirant who has deep respect for his or her Master is the fortunate one. The seeker who digs a deep well in one place is far more likely to find water than one who digs several shallow wells in different places.

7.21 "Due to ignorance you say that I am a Master and you are an aspirant, but in fact the reality is you!"

As long as you confuse the Self with the body, you are liable to think of the Master as a body also. However, one thing you can be sure of is that the Master does not perceive any difference between your essential being and his. He knows that the Self is the only reality and that you are That, just as he is. Both are waves on the same ocean. For the aspirant who still perceives duality, the apparent distance can be removed by devotion. Here is what Kabir says:

My Guru is in Benares,
I am on the seashore,
But God knows that the Guru is not absent from my heart
Even for an instant.

7.22 "When a saint dies he doesn't worry because he doesn't exist and he doesn't carry these (good and bad) thoughts with him."

When you are deeply asleep you rest quite happily, forgetting the world. Troubles only come back when the ego is there again, when you wake in the morning. The Master doesn't worry about death because anything in him that can die is already dead. He knows that death is just like deep sleep. For him, it will be the final rest after so many births, so many revolutions in the circle of ignorance. Everybody welcomes sleep at the end of the day and makes a comfortable bed in order to enjoy it! Death is likewise not to be feared. It is the ego that fears death because it knows that thoughts do not remain in deep sleep and that it is itself only a thought. The ego stores up judgments of good and bad and harbors desires that remain unfulfilled. These desires are the seed of another birth.

7.23 "The Master plays with the concepts like a child plays with toys."

Maharaj often spoke with humor. When he was talking, there was an undercurrent of joy and playfulness that was very infectious. Often, everyone in the room would be laughing at something he said. I use the word "playfulness" because I don't have a better way to describe that sense of lightness that he had. It was very like the feeling you get around a small child, who is playing without a care in the world. Concepts are like toy building-blocks. It is fun to put them together and make some structure out of them, and then to forget it and make something new.

7.24 "Master shows how to put an end, how to solve that theorem, but you have to solve it for yourself."

One wonderful thing about having a teacher is that you know that you can ask. In a school, the teacher explains something on the blackboard and then says, "Now you do it," but if you get stuck, you can still raise your hand and get help. In the end, you have to solve the problem yourself—you have to get that moment of understanding that can only come through your own efforts—but you can get a lot of help up to that point. If the teacher leaned over your shoulder in class and solved the theorem for you, it would be no use to you because you would not understand the solution and could not repeat it. So asking questions is good, but you have to arrive at the final understanding by yourself.

7.25 "Knowledge or thought is the greatest ignorance, and only the Master can tell you that."

Which "I" is going to know reality? Can the picture see the screen? If you meet a teacher who says "I am enlightened," or "You are ignorant," run from them as fast as you can! Only the real Master will tell you that the I-thought is the root of illusion and unhappiness. He will therefore constantly point to the fact that what you are is the reality that is beyond knowledge, beyond the concept of "I" as an individual. He will tell you that there is no difference between Master and disciple, except that the disciple is holding onto the wrong belief that he or she is ignorant. The Master is not out to gain anything and will not make any false promises or offer any guarantees.

7.26 "Master makes you bigger and bigger. You are all. Then you feel you've become enlightened, you feel joy."

On the way to final understanding, you may get different experiences of temporary awakening or enlightenment. They may last for hours, days, or weeks. Maharaj describes this kind of experience here. You feel that you have expanded to include everything, you are the creator of the world, you feel profound joy and peace. An experience like this is of course a very good sign of progress. You may regard it as a blessing from the Master (who is within you). However, it is just an experience and, because it is an experience, it is temporary. It is easy to confuse a profound spiritual experience with realization.

7.27 "Then the Master says you have not understood. Nothing is true."

During a profound spiritual experience, the ego may be temporarily overwhelmed, but it is still there in the background. For example, you feel "I am the creator of the world," "I am experiencing bliss," and so on. After a while, the experience fades and you start to worry that you will lose that state. This can be very painful because, from the point of view of the ego, something very desirable is being lost. In the world of duality, what goes up, must come down.

The Master will tell you that you have not fully understood. Reality, the Self, does not depend on any kind of experience whatever. No experience can be true, because it appears and disappears. You, the Self, remain always.

7.28 "You get your wallet back, but it was already yours."

Maharaj used to say that gaining Self-knowledge is like finding the wallet you had lost. You don't gain anything that was not already yours. This is really the central point in *Advaita Vedanta*. If Self-knowledge is not something that you already have, it must be an object that can come into existence at some point. If it can come into existence, it can also go out of existence again, which means it is temporary and so is not worth pursuing. Therefore, you must already have Self-knowledge. The only obstacle is the belief that you do not have it. The Master's work is to remove this ignorance.

7.29 "It depends upon you and how much you accept. Accept in the right way and you will say bye-bye to the Master."

The ability to accept what the Master says is a power. Each disciple comes to the Master with a different power to accept. It is exactly like degrees of ripeness. No one can say why it is so. The Master is willing to repeat his teaching over and over for the benefit of those disciples whose power is developing. Others will only need to hear a few times and they will be able to accept it in the right way. The last stages of the process of ripening happen within, with the disciple coming to the understanding that he or she is not separate from the Master, and that the Master is his or her own Self.

In the final understanding, the Self absorbs the separate "I" of the disciple into Itself and the process of Self-seeking comes to an end. Once the fruit is ripe, it falls from the tree, and, once it has fallen, it cannot go back again. The disciple then has no further need for the Master's teaching, and, in the tradition of *Vedanta*, is actively encouraged to leave the Master's presence. This is because a tree growing up in the shade of a larger tree will not develop its own strength. It needs to be out in the sun and rain and send out its own roots and branches. So the disciple says goodbye to the Master, but however far he or she goes, never forgets the one who gave the gift of knowledge.

7.30 "All are nothing but bubbles on the ocean. Master helps to break your bubble by understanding, that's all."

The ego is the bubble on the ocean of the Self. It is so small, so fragile. It appears, only to disappear momentarily, having no substance of its own. It is nothing but water and yet it separates that tiny portion of the vast ocean and makes it feel alone and apart from the rest. The ego is only there so that it can be broken and the Self can be one again. That is the work of the Master. He helps you break that bubble of the ego that is nothing, but which appears to separate you from your Self. Then you return consciously to what you always have been and you merge into the deep peace of the endless ocean of being.

7.31 "If you want the reality, take as much as you want, but if you want zero, I've got nothing to give you."

This sentence is a good summary of the work of the Master. The Master is a pointer to the reality that is yourself. You can use his teaching to eliminate your wrong ideas about yourself, to focus on that reality, and, finally, to realize the Self that you already are. The Master facilitates the whole wonderful process of discovery, but it is a process that goes on in you. You have to reach out and take what is being offered, verify it for yourself by meditation and reflection, and make it into your own understanding, so that it changes you completely.

That is how it seems as you tread the path. In the end, however, you realize that the Master was within you all the time, drawing you to

Him, and at the same time appearing in physical form to instruct and encourage you.

Here is a final verse from Kabir:

When I was conscious of my individual existence,
The love of the Guru was absent in me.
When the love of the guru filled my heart,
My lesser self was displaced.
O Kabir, this path is too narrow for two to travel.

8

August: Grace and Understanding

8.1 "What the Master says, accept it, That is the grace."

When you are a seeker, you are impelled by a power that is not in your control. You have no choice but to seek the Self because nothing else will satisfy you. You are aware of this power and you want to spend time with other seekers who are also aware of it. That power is called grace. It is actually the divine power of pure consciousness, not separate from *Brahman*. Grace is God. Everyone and everything is animated by this same power, only some are more conscious of it than others. The ability to accept what the Master says shows that the mind is becoming more transparent and offering less resistance to grace.

8.2 "Nothing is to be done, only understanding is required."

If you look at the tower of an Indian temple or the spire of a cathedral, you can see that it is built in stages, wider at the base and then tapering to a point at the top. Understanding is like that; encompassing many, sometimes contradictory ideas in the beginning, but focused in the end on a single reality. The final understanding is the knowledge of the Self, in which all understanding is included. To reach Self-knowledge, doing and the concept of doership have to be set aside. Understanding comes through surrender to the power of grace that is working in you.

8.3 "Accept what the Master says and you will always be at rest."

The way to Self-knowledge is a path of increasing peace and harmony. Contradictions are banished as you focus your attention on understanding the truths embodied in the Master's teaching. You feel more grace as you open yourself up to it. Grace is always there. Sri Ramakrishna said that the wind of grace is always blowing, you just need to put up a sail.

8.4 "If a plane is late, say it is my choice, it is my order."

One of the results of increasing surrender or opening to divine grace, is that you worry less about what happens or what will happen. There is an intuitive recognition that what happens is intended to happen and that no harm will come to you. In this frame of mind, when you are at the airport and the plane is late, you say "I am happy with this, it is all for the good." You do not resist what happens, you just accept it. The realized person, who knows himself or herself to be one with the divine power, can also say "It is my choice, it is my order." For the realized person, there is no personal will or desire and so what happens is always "my choice," whatever it is.

8.5 "Take everything on yourself, Don't blame others."

If you become angry with someone else, you are the loser, because you lose your peace of mind. You may feel justified, but by expressing your anger, you are giving in to the ego's view of the world, in which everything has to be arranged for its comfort and convenience. It is better to take the blame yourself, say "It was something I did that was wrong," and keep your peace of mind. The ego will never accept things as they are because it would have no scope for fulfilling the desires that keep it alive. Anger and blaming others are therefore very common negative emotions that help to sustain the ego.

8.6 "Play your part, no harm, but understand "I am not this. I am He."

A statement about the way the realized person sees the world becomes an instruction for the aspirant. Maharaj often spoke in this way. This statement is an example. The realized person knows beyond any doubt "I am He." The instruction to the aspirant is "Understand that you are He." By adopting the way of thinking of the Master, the aspirant grows into that understanding. In this case, the Master knows he is playing a part and that the play is already written. Why should he be concerned with it? He acts his part but knows it doesn't make any difference to worry or to imagine that the outcome can be changed. Therefore he offers this attitude to calm the aspirant's mind.

8.7 "Accept what happens. Don't fight with what comes. In this way, the ego will dissolve."

Calmness and clarity of mind are important preconditions for Self-knowledge. The mind is easily agitated by wanting things to be other than what they are. Acceptance of what happens is therefore a powerful means to weaken the ego. Acceptance happens through grace. One way that the ego sustains itself is by constantly trying to impose its desires on what is spontaneously happening. There is an old rhyme that describes the situation:

As a rule, man is a fool.
When it's hot, he wants it cool.
When it's cool, he wants it hot.
Always wanting what is not.

8.8 "Forget all limitations and be He, the reality."

You are He already, so if you do not feel that is the case, it is because of some false concept in the mind. Efforts are always to get rid of what is not true. There is never any need to become what you already are. False concepts such as "I am the body," and doubts such as "How can I be He?" are the unnecessary limitations that Maharaj says to forget. They are like a layer of dust on the surface of the clear water of the mind, which in its true nature is pure consciousness. Remove the dust and the Self is reflected clearly and experienced as unlimited being.

8.9 "Break down the walls of your mind, and you become the sky."

You are already the pure knowledge pervading everywhere. Boundaries and divisions are imaginary. Space is everywhere the same. If it is inside a room or inside a jar, it is still space. The apparent difference is in the mind only. Through identification with the body, there is a feeling of separateness and limitation, as though the space in the room were to say "I have become imprisoned within these four walls." Space is space, inside and outside, but if it imagines itself imprisoned, it will feel that way. This is how the ego works. The understanding must come that, just as the walls are not a limitation to space, the body cannot limit the Self. What is all-pervasive cannot be confined.

8.10 "If troubles happen to you, take for granted that it is for the best."

Everything happens according to the natural operation of the divine law, which some call the will of God. If you are an aspirant, grace is already working in you and around you, and you can be sure that events will arrange themselves so that your aspiration will deepen and strengthen. This is the nature of the divine law. Sometimes, this means that difficult situations present themselves or troubles come when you least expect them. However, difficulties generally provide an opportunity to increase detachment from worldly things or to surrender more fully to the divine will, and so they are positive experiences. There is a Nepali saying: "All obstacles are blessings from the guru."

8.11 "The understanding should be so strong that it should not be broken by any thought."

Maharaj is indicating here the goal of practice. The basic principle or method of realization is that once you have heard the truth "I am He" from the Master, you keep that truth in mind and revert to it whenever other thoughts intervene. First there is hearing (*shravana*), then meditation/contemplation (*dhyana*), and finally Self-knowledge (*jnana*). You keep your mind focused on Him until you realize Him. This is the path of devotion (*bhakti yoga*). In the process, you enquire and find out "who am I?" leaving aside everything you are not. So this is also the path of knowledge (*jnana yoga*). After realization occurs, your mind naturally reverts to Him. Even though you are occupied in some task, as soon as you stop that activity, you find that you are already resting in Him. Understanding is never interrupted. When this happens, there is nothing left to be done.

8.12 "You have to understand without the mind."

This is another description of the experience of the realized person. The great teacher of classical *Vedanta*, Swami Dayananda, said that Understanding or knowledge comes in the mind and is of the mind, but Self-knowledge or Self-realization comes in the mind but is not *of* the mind. We all know the experience of understanding something one day and being able to express that understanding, but then, the next day, we feel that we no longer understand that idea and cannot express it with conviction. What has happened to the understanding that was there yesterday? Understanding, being based on knowledge, can be obscured by the clouds of ignorance. This is why realization is emphasized. When there is realization of the Self, there is no ignorance to obscure understanding. Understanding does not appear and disappear, but remains constant. Only then is there 100% conviction. That understanding is without the mind.

8.13 "If your mind gets changed then you can understand anything, why not?"

Maharaj often said that the Master changes your mind. The mind is so important because the whole picture of the world is contained in it. The world is in you, you are not in the world. Change the mind and the picture changes as well. When realization occurs, you find that you can understand anything. The Master's ideas which before seemed obscure are now crystal clear. Why? Because you are seeing from the same point of view that the Master sees from. In fact, you and He are one.

8.14 "When you understand your own power, you will say that everything is your choice."

Everything is in you. All experiences take place within your consciousness. Therefore, what you see belongs to you and is your own creation. This is what it means to be all-pervasive; you know that without you, nothing is. If you see this, then you understand that what happens is happening by itself; you are there and events are coming and going in your presence. Will you try to interfere and have things go one way rather than another? If you act, you act, if you don't act, you don't act, but, whatever happens, you do not imagine that you are the doer. You say that it is my choice and you accept things as they are.

8.15 "He who understands, gets rid of everything."

Nothing disturbs the peace of the Self. Whether it is known or unknown, it remains as It is. The Self is all that really exists. Everything else is a show that comes and goes. When the seeker finds the Self, he or she gets rid of everything else. Transitory objects become of no importance.

The following verse is from the poet Rahim, who lived at the court of the Emperor Akbar in the sixteenth century:

Heart is emptied of longings,
All the anxieties are gone.
Those who covet not a thing
Are the masters of the world.

8.16 "Ignorance prevails in you, so take out that ignorance by accepting what the Master says. That is the grace."

Grace is there in the beginning, in the middle, and in the end of the search. Nothing is accomplished without grace because grace is the divine power that animates every being and, in due course, draws those beings back to their source. Ignorance persists right up till the end of the search, when the seeker finds that the Self is already realized and, in fact, is not other than the seeker. All of this happens by the gradual removal of ignorance through acceptance and understanding of the Master's teaching. The desire to find the Self is grace, meeting the Master is grace, acceptance of his teaching is grace. All happens in the Self, which is the source of grace.

8.17 "Only the power of understanding can defeat the ego."

In the *Mahabharata*, the Kauravas chose Lord Krishna's armies but the Pandavas chose Lord Krishna Himself. The ego wants possessions, worldly things, but the true seeker wants only understanding, because the light of understanding is the only thing that can dispel the darkness of ignorance. Understanding is an inner transformation, a change of mind, which is what is needed because the ego is nothing but a habitual way of thinking.

Understanding is really a rather mysterious thing. It is not just knowledge. You may have to hear a particular teaching many times before you can say that you understand it. Understanding does accumulate over time—if you look back on how you understand an idea today compared to how you understood it a couple of years ago, you will surely see the difference—but, as long as you are an aspirant, understanding is not as reliable as money in the bank. You never know, when you wake up in the morning, what your understanding will be like. One day, you may feel that you understand very much, but the next day you may feel that you don't understand anything. It is like the weather: it is changeable and not within your control. The life of the seeker is really the story of the changing pattern of darkness and light caused by the confrontation between the ego and the power of understanding. In the early stages, the struggle seems fairly even, but as time goes on, understanding groups itself and asserts itself while the ego retires and retreats. In the end, the power of understanding, which is also the power of grace, is absolutely triumphant.

8.18 "Sat-chit-ananda is not the final understanding, but if you want to go to the fortieth floor, you have to go up to the thirty-ninth, no?"

In this tradition, the final understanding, or final reality, is *Parabrahman*, which eternally exists without expression or manifestation. Manifestation begins when you say "I am," and that is *sat-chit-ananda*. *Sat-chit-ananda* means experience—it is the original experience of differentiation from which all else unfolds. *Sat-chit-ananda* is the ultimate statement that can be made about reality, but it is still a statement that uses words and so is relative, not absolute. This is why Maharaj says that it is the thirty-ninth floor, not the fortieth. Nothing whatever can be said about the final reality.

Jnaneshwar devotes the fifth chapter of the *Amritanubhav* to a discussion of the *sat-chit-ananda* triad. Here is a short extract:

These well-know words, "chit," "sat," and "ananda,"
Are popularly used, it is true;

But when the knower becomes one with That to which they refer,
Then they vanish
As the clouds that pour down as rain,
Or like the rivers which flow into the sea,
Or like a journey when one's destination is reached.

8.19 "When you hear a song, understand that I am writer and the singer."

What is that power that creates in any musician, painter, writer, or artist? It is the power of *sat-chit-ananda* that is playing in everything. That power makes the child play and the writer write. The power is not different from life itself. Life is not a mechanical force that operates without feeling; it is full of *ananda*, which is love without an object. That love expresses itself through many forms: in the listener as well as in the singer, in the feeling evoked as well as in the song that evokes it. When you know the Self, you know that that power is yourself and that it is also everywhere.

8.20 "When you understand that thought is wrong, that is the thoughtless reality."

If thought was true or real, it would never go away. It would have life of its own and be under no one's control. You hear about cases of mentally ill people who hear "voices in my head," which tell them to do things that no sane person would ever do. Normally, thought is not like that. Thought is more of a temporary displacement of the natural stillness of the mind. In deep sleep, that natural stillness is experienced, which is why everyone welcomes sleep at the end of the day, which has usually been dominated by thought-driven activities. Thought has to be taken as "wrong" because you generally think it is "right," that is, that it is *you*. When you break that habit of wrong identification of the Self with thought, the thoughtless reality is already there.

8.21 "Know your mind and you are He. That is the final understanding."

You can easily confuse the Self with thinking, although they are not at all the same. Thinking is not your true nature. A traditional example is a red-hot iron ball, in which the iron takes on the characteristics of fire, while the fire takes the form of the ball. The fire is the Self and the ball is thought. As long as you take yourself to be the thoughts, you cannot know the Self as it is, that is, without the form of thinking. The Self is formless and can exist without a form. Thought is form and cannot exist apart from the Self. To know the mind, you have to realize that you are beyond the mind. Then you are He.

8.22 "If you want to be realized, you have to throw off the mind. You must want it, and give your life to it, otherwise it is of no use."

No one is going to argue with you if you want to see the world as having a solid, objective, reality. Likewise, no one will object if you want to take the ego to be real, as modern psychology does. No one follows a spiritual path for the sake of finding "truth" for its own sake, but for the sake of finding personal satisfaction and fulfillment. Seeking begins because you are not satisfied with your conception of the world and, in particular, with your conception of yourself. Something is missing, something is not correct, and life is dissatisfying as a result. When you feel that absence, then you start to want the truth more than you want other things.

When you meet the Master, you get confirmation that your conception of yourself is wrong. You *are* taking yourself to be something you are not. Then you understand you have to throw off the ego-mind. But how? Can the ego destroy itself? From that point on, you are engaged in a life-and-death struggle of heroic proportions, in which illusion battles against the power and light of reality to retain its hold on the mind. It has as much chance of victory as Ravanna had against Rama, or the Kauravas against Lord Krishna. The result is a foregone conclusion. The campaign can go on a long time or it can be over quickly, depending on how much you want final understanding and how much time and energy you commit to it, because it is a law that everything has to be paid for.

8.23 "Once you've reached the destination, where is the need for understanding? You're at the fortieth floor, what to understand?"

Struggle and effort does not go on for ever. There is a goal and an end to seeking. It is true that that goal does not involve gaining an object or acquiring anything that was not already yours. But it is still an attainment, in the sense that the end of a journey is an attainment. You arrive at a destination that you immediately recognize. You come home. Then where is there to go? Wherever you look, there you are. What is there to do? There is no doer. What is there to understand? There are no questions.

8.24 "Understanding is a great thing, but that understanding is finally untrue, because it only knows 'that which is not.'"

You cannot have any understanding of the Self, because you are That, and you cannot step outside of yourself in order to understand yourself. Understanding has to be of some object. This is why understanding is finally untrue. Anything that is an object appears and disappears and so "is not." Understanding of the Master's teaching is essential along the way, but there is no understanding in the final reality.

8.25 "Saints say that you can ask for anything you want. I can give you, but you must have the power to accept."

Christ said: "The harvest is plentiful, but the laborers are few." There is no shortage of teachers but there are always very few who are ready to accept what is offered. It seems to be normal for only a handful of disciples of a Master to become Masters themselves in the same lifetime. The Master is ready to give the knowledge that leads to the final understanding, but the disciple must be prepared to receive it and to assimilate it. Any limitations are on the receiving side, not on the side of the giver. The disciple must adjust his or her frequency upwards to be able to receive the Master's message.

8.26 "You must understand your own mind. Mind is the only factor."

Mind is both the means to Self-realization and the obstacle to it. Hence, Maharaj says that the mind is the only factor. There is nothing outside of your own mind that prevents you merging in the peace of your own true being. Neither is there anything outside of your own mind that can accept the Master's words. The Master, who is your own Self, stands beyond the mind. Nevertheless, it is the mind that must attune itself to the new understanding coming from the Master. When the mind becomes perfectly attuned to understanding, the mind itself becomes transparent and there is no separation from the source of understanding.

8.27 "Everything depends on your capability, or capacity to accept."

The Master can give knowledge, but not understanding. If understanding were the same as knowledge, you would only have to hear the Master's teaching once to have final understanding and become enlightened. This doesn't happen because understanding is actually a combination of knowledge and your entire being; that is to say, knowledge cannot be accepted just by the intellect—it must be accepted by the heart and by the senses as well. So, for example, when you hear the idea "I am He," you really accept it when you not only see the inevitable logic of it, but feel and sense its profound emotional rightness at the same time. Understanding is so important because it is only understanding that has the power to fundamentally change the mind and clear it of the dust of ignorance.

8.28 "Move ahead slowly. Slowly one can get it, why not?"

The old fable of the race between the tortoise and the hare expresses the truth that slow but steady progress is better than rapid progress that is not sustained. The hare feels that he is so far ahead that he stops to take a nap. While he is sleeping, the tortoise passes him by and crosses the finish line first. A steady pressure combined with faith in the Master and an unassuming attitude are the best ways to increase understanding and defeat the ego.

8.29 "Think of yourself! Don't think of others. There is nobody there except you."

It is a waste of time to try to imagine how other people are progressing relative to yourself, or to make judgements about what they are doing. You cannot know others and you only end up projecting your own theories onto them. In fact, the perception of "others" as separate, self-motivated beings is itself false. It is an illusion that persists as long as you think of yourself in that way. Actually, you are living in, and as, the current of divine wisdom at this very moment. That power is your true nature. You are really the ground of your experiences and not the experiences themselves or the experiencer of them. When you think about yourself and feel what you really are, you see that you are the only One, the One that is playing in everything and everyone. You are aware of yourself everywhere. When you see "others," you see only yourself reflected in them. Then there is no fear and no judgement.

8.30 "When you have understanding, mind becomes satisfied, no thoughts come."

On the way to the final understanding comes much peace. The mind becomes relatively quiet. But even though the journey becomes increasingly beautiful, there is still the sense that the end of the journey has not been reached and you don't know how long it will take. Until that final understanding comes, you cannot have complete satisfaction. That is how things are arranged. Life is intended for that complete satisfaction and nothing less than that will fully satisfy.

"Satisfaction" as a goal may not seem very exciting compared to "bliss" or "love," but what is bliss but absence of desire and freedom from longing? When there is understanding, you realize that you have no need for anything. Then wanting subsides and the mind becomes your servant.

8.31 "This knowledge can be understood by the grace of the Master, nothing else."

When you first receive the Master's teaching, the mind begins to think about reality and starts to become detached from wordly objects. That is the result of the power of grace. As the mind turns inward and draws closer to its source, that also is the operation of grace. When the Master, the Self, finally makes you one with Him, that is His grace again. Grace is present in the beginning, the middle, and the end. It is the Master's grace, because the Master is all there is. He is within you and without you, He is the teacher and the disciple, the seeker and the object of seeking, the source and the goal. Life fulfills its purpose when the Self, which had become two, becomes One again. In that final understanding, there is no longer any individual and no longer anything to understand.

9

September: Devotion

9.1 "I and the Master are one."

The realized person is always having the *darshan* of God in his heart or her heart. The experience of being one with God is contained there. Devotion is a flame that is always burning in the temple of the body. Devotion is natural and, paradoxically, it is One, not two. "The Master and I are one" means that the whole process of worship has become Self-contained—there is no external object of reverence. The Master is known as yourself. What does this feel like? It is a state of complete satisfaction and contentment. When you know that the source of happiness is yourself, why would you look for happiness anywhere else? With this understanding, all the troubles of the world fade into the background and cease to bother you. Your whole life is integrated, focused on the Self. Saint Tukaram wrote:

Like the bee, only interested in honey from the flower, he is always thinking of the Self. Inside and outside, only Self.

9.2 "Say there is nothing bad in the world. That is love."

This statement is impossible to understand through the ego-mind. The mind will point to many things in the world that are "bad," not just things which are undesirable, but things which appear to indicate that the world itself is a cold and harsh place, a Hell rather than a Heaven. By dwelling on negative images, the ego strengthens its feeling of separation and justifies its selfish point of view.

In reality, there is nothing bad in the world because there is nothing at all that exists independently of the one who is seeing it. Wherever you look, you are only seeing yourself. When you look in a mirror, you know that what you are seeing is yourself, that is, it is yourself as you appear, but not the actual being who is the source of the reflection. If the mirror is cracked or dirty, you don't imagine that "you" are affected by that. Even if your reflection is not pretty, you continue to love yourself, to cherish your own existence. Nothing changes the love that you feel at the center of your being. When you feel this love clearly, when you know it to be yourself, then you see it everywhere. You do not feel anything to be "bad."

9.3 "Forget everything and you are there. Where are you not?"

There is no real difference between *bhakti* (devotion) and *jnana* (knowledge). You can say "He is everywhere" and worship the all-pervasive beauty of the divine power, but Self-knowledge tells you that "You are He," and so you know that it is yourself that you see everywhere and so it is yourself that you are worshipping. This understanding comes when the ego-mind has been forgotten. You remain in your formless and limitless condition, just as the space remains when the walls of the building have been demolished.

9.4 "When the piece of salt dissolves, it becomes ocean."

Saint Tukaram wrote:

Once in water, salt cannot return to solid form.
Likewise, the one who has understood reality is dissolved.
Thought has become thoughtless.
The Saint stays in Brahman.
He never goes again into the illusion.

When the mind is active and thoughts are following one another rapidly, you cannot be aware of the peace that is natural to the Self. When thoughts subside, for example, in a state of meditation, that peace is experienced directly as your own being. It is just like the salt dissolving in the ocean. Thought has become thoughtless and you remain as that thoughtless reality. Thoughts may still arise but they are not seen as separate from the Self and so do not disturb that peace. When thoughts arise, the Self *is*. When thoughts subside, the Self *is*. The thoughts are not like fish, which have their own lives to live, but like the waves which come and go on the surface of the ocean and are a part of it.

9.5 "Who will see Him and by which eyes can you look at Him?"

Where is reality? Can you find it somewhere "out there?" If "you" could find it, it would be an object to you and then who would "you" be? You would have to be something separate from reality to be able to look at it. That cannot be. You, yourself, must be reality. You can look at the world but you can never look at yourself, you can never make yourself into an object. "You," "He," "I," are just concepts, word-labels that are used to divide the indivisible so that verbal communication can take place. There is One reality and it never comes out of itself to make two, even though the whole world appears. Nothing in the world appearance can see that reality that makes everything possible. Can the characters in the movie see the screen on which they are projected?

9.6 "There is only oneness, so whatever you see and perceive is He."

You cannot see your own eyes, but you can see their reflection if you have a mirror. The manifest universe is a mirror of light in which the being of the Self is reflected. There is nothing which is not the Self, but the Self is not contained in the manifestation any more than the person is contained in the reflection in the mirror.

The reflection is seen by means of rays of light. Energy and matter, the three dimensions of space, and the dimension of time appear there. It is all a show of movement, power, activity, and differentiation—the play of *Maya*, of consciousness. In reality, there is only oneness, so whatever you see and perceive is That alone, and the apparent multiplicity is nothing but illusion. The reflection is real to the extent that it has reality as its source, but it has no independent existence. In the process of Self-understanding, you first reject the world as untrue and affirm only the source as reality. Then, later, when Self-knowledge is there, you see the world as yourself and you accept it as partaking of your own reality. Then, whether you say "everything is He" or "everything is myself," you have reached the highest level of devotion. The following verse from one of the bhajans sung in this tradition expresses this *uttamabhakti* (highest devotion):

Concentrate on Him, outside and inside pervading everywhere, your own Self, ever-shining, ever-ready, self-effulgent, ever-pure, ever-present before you.

9.7 "Be faithful to the Master, That's why you worship."

Whether you do specific devotional practices, such as daily puja and bhajans or whether your worship is more of an inner attitude of surrender, devotion is essential, both before and after Self-realization. In both cases, the reason for devotion is the same—to be faithful to the Master. The only difference is that after realization, there is the understanding that the Master is yourself. Devotion is then simply a manifestation of the faithfulness that is already there. Before realization, devotion is a fundamental means of sustaining that faithfulness. It is part of the method of the way of understanding, because it is essential to keep the mind focused on what is important. It is equally important to surrender to the Master. The mind should shift into a rhythm in which life revolves around the expression of faithfulness to the Master.

9.8 "You and the Master are one, but still as long as you are in body, you must worship."

Devotion is not optional. Whether you consider yourself to be a devotee or whether you go by the path of knowledge (*jnana*), any form of spiritual practice requires that you be devoted to God, or the guru, or whatever it is that you conceive of as worthy of your love and aspiration. To study the Master's teachings means you have to be devoted to him or her. To chant the name of the Lord means you must be devoted to That which the name represents. The fact that you are already the Self, already one with the Master, and even the presence of the understanding that comes with Self-knowledge, does not change the need for devotion. To be in the human form and to have a human mind that recognizes reality means that devotion is a natural response.

The body eats to give itself strength. The mind studies to gain understanding. The heart seeks out companions to gain support. The body, heart, and mind must work together to maintain the right relationship with the divine power. "Right relationship" means for the aspirant in the first place not forgetting that that power is supreme, and for the *jnani* (realized person) it signifies the natural relationship between the lower nature and the higher, both of which are known to be ones's own Self. To the ego, which is ignorance, it seems contradictory that there can be a relationship in oneness, but it is the thought of contradiction itself that creates the disturbance. The feeling of devotion which is both dual and non-dual continues without any sense of contradiction. Kabir wrote:

Kabir has washed off the dirt of ignorance
With the water of devotion;
A day passed without devotion

Is passed in a tomb.

9.9 "Master says accept everything with love and gratitude, not just good things."

The attitude of devotion is the attitude of acceptance. "Who am I to reject what comes to me?" Whatever happens is given by a higher power than this limited mind. However, it is not given in an arbitrary way, but as the result of past actions. God is the giver of *karmaphala*, the fruits of action. Whatever happens is therefore necessary. The illusory ego conceives the desire to accept some things, which it labels "good," and to reject others, which it labels "bad." Devotion to the Master, to God, to the Self, brings with it the power to accept whatever happens in the right way, with increasing love and gratitude.

9.10 "You are He. So whom to love and whom not to love?"

The love that is real love is not concerned with any object. It doesn't need anything and, in any case, there is nothing to get. Talk of love is false when it is talk of the love of one person for another. In the myth of Narcissus, a handsome young man sees his reflection in the still water of a pool and falls in love with it. This story means that the world is attractive and absorbing as long as you are ignorant of your true Self, the One who is causing the reflection.

In ignorance, you imagine that you are someone and that you can love what you see. You ascribe independent existence to the "I" that has appeared and you assume that all the emotions that come to the "I" are true. In fact, you are enchanted by your own projection, hypnotized by the image you find yourself gazing at. To break the spell, you must turn your gaze away from the reflection and toward the source. Then you begin to understand that love does not have an object, but it is what you already *are*. There is no possibility of loving this one and not that one, because you are already existing as the beloved Self in everything that lives.

9.11 "Be like an animal that waits for things to come into its mouth."

The Master is like a person who is very deeply asleep. He doesn't care for the world because he knows it is a dream. He doesn't try to initiate any actions. He just lets things unfold. Whatever comes, he deals with, but he does not identify with the result. What he does, he does for its own sake, not for the sake of something else. A *sadhu* (renunciate) takes food only when it is freely offered to him. The Master is the greatest *sadhu* because his whole life is lived like that. Whatever comes to him, he accepts it as *prasad* from the Lord.

9.12 "Purity of mind is nothing other than forgetting the mind, for it doesn't exist."

Reality is non-dual, whereas the mind is dual in nature. The mind is based on the thought "I," and when there is "I" there is also "not-I." The mind thinks in terms of good and bad, positive and negative, purity and impurity. The world conceived by the mind can never be all one thing—all good for example—because the dualistic nature of the mind will always compare one thing to another, set one thing against another. The world created by the mind is made up of relative views, of ideals, and of value judgments. It is a conceptual, interpreted world. Real purity exists before any of this even arises. That reality has nothing to do with concepts of what is pure or impure. It is neutral with regard to the relative world, that is, it is beyond the opposites. The mind does not exist there.

9.13 "The Master is everywhere. He is never away from you. You and he are one."

"Master" is really another word for consciousness or God. When you see the Master sitting in front of you during *satsang*, there is actually nobody there. There is nobody where you take yourself to be either, just your thoughts and the underlying assumption that there is a person who has independent existence, desires this or that, is the doer, and so on. All this is imagination. The Master is everywhere. There is no difference between what the Master is and what you are, just as there is no difference between the space in this room and the space in the next room. The walls and windows don't limit space. It is all-pervasive. In the same way, the Master, consciousness, is not affected by the overlaying concepts of "I" and "you." These mental boundaries are apparent, not real.

9.14 "A thought comes in the mind and the heart gives force, power to it. So heart is power, it is life."

Everyone is devoted to something. Worship is action that expresses what it is that an individual values. One person may worship fast cars, another worships ambition or security. Wherever the source of happiness is perceived, that is where the heart places its attention and affection. All creatures seek happiness and so all are seeking the same thing. The same principle of seeking operates in the worldly person and in the spiritual person. The only difference is in the object of affection. The spiritual seeker understands that external objects cannot give real happiness and so seeks for the source within. Others continue to seek outside.

A thought comes in the mind and the heart gives power to it. Emotion arises and so you say "Yes, I want that!" Emotion is movement. When the waking state appears in the morning, did you ask it to come? No, it appears as a movement that wakes the mind. What was still, undisturbed, stirs itself and moves into relationship with the world of its own projection. There is a desire to experience the world again. This goes on for some time until the force is spent. Then there is a desire to return to the deep sleep state. This cycle of desire, fulfilment, and disillusion is the operation of the divine power that lives in the heart of every being. Christ said: "Life is a movement and a rest." Life itself is an interlude, a lucid interval between two periods of oblivion, a spark of remembering between two poles of forgetfulness.

9.15 "When his body goes away, the Master remains with you in your heart by understanding."

If someone gives you a gift, when you look at the gift, you remember who gave it to you. The Master gives you understanding, so when you experience your understanding, you remember him. Love and gratitude arises naturally. In this way, the mind, which has become purified by surrender to the Master, acknowledges the origin of the knowledge that has transformed it. The true disciple, even when he or she becomes a Master, always has the attitude "Everything I got, I got from my Master," and continues to have the attitude of a servant. In this way, the purity of the lineage is maintained, and the teaching is passed on from guru to disciple, and from one generation to the next.

9.16 "When you meet a saint, he makes you a saint."

When you meet a guru whom you consider to be a saint, and whom you feel is the right teacher for you, then, automatically, you try to be as much like him or her as possible. At the same time, the Master is telling you that there is no difference between you and him. You are not an ant, crawling on the ground, but a bird, able to fly freely without limitation.

Disciples differ in their ability to accept and understand what the Master is saying. Those who are ready to accept, become Masters themselves. By giving up their self-will to the Master, they make themselves empty. Then the Master within can take over.

9.17 "God is dwelling in the innermost heart of all beings and receiving different kinds of service rendered to Himself." (Sri Siddharameshwar Maharaj)

Note: Maharaj did not say a great deal about devotion himself. However, because the subject is very important, we have made up the number of days for the month with a series of quotations from Maharaj's Master, Sri Siddharameshwar Maharaj.

Whatever deity or whichever guru you feel you are worshipping, it is in fact only the divine power that is manifest as both the worshipper and the object of worship. God is light and love and is present everywhere. The human mind acts as a prism, splitting the pure, white light into different colors and creating the different forms of gods and gurus. He is receiving all kinds of devotion and service, but the joke is that He is also offering it.

9.18 "His worship consists in knowing that he is always present, eternal." (Sri Siddharameshwar Maharaj)

You cannot worship the formless (*nirguna*) reality directly. You have to worship indirectly, by means of a form (*saguna*). To worship the form of the Master, or of a god or goddess, is a convenient way of worshipping the One, all-pervasive, and eternal Self. When you look at the image you are worshipping, you know that He is everpresent everywhere. The object of worship—the picture of the guru or the statue of the deity—that is there in front of you, is a symbol that represents the Self, but at the same time, the Self cannot be worshipped without its representation. Therefore, in worshipping, there is really no difference between *saguna* and *nirguna*, between manifest and unmanifest. This understanding need not be confined to formal worship. The whole of the manifest universe is a representation of Him. Saint Tukaram wrote:

Saguna and nirguna are One.
This understanding came to Tukaram
Whatever you see and perceive is Me.

9.19 "After realization of the Self, the aspirant regards his Master as the greatest of all. He feels that he belongs to the Master." (Sri Siddharameshwar Maharaj)

In this tradition, the aspirant allies himself or herself to a long lineage of Masters, in which devotion to the guru as the symbol of the Self is of primary importance. This allegiance opens the aspirant to the influence of Masters other than his or her immediate guru. This tradition also stresses the value of continuing with devotion after realization. When enlightenment occurs, the aspirant is free from limitation and there is no obligation to anyone or anything. However, there is also the understanding that Self-realization is really nothing but the fruition of the seed that was planted by the Master, who got it from his Master, and so on. He belongs to that lineage and at the same time to the Master who is within all. By equating the Master with the Self, the aspirant is simply acknowledging that there is no doer but the divine power of the Self.

9.20 "Our only duty is worship of the sadguru." (Sri Siddharameshwar Maharaj)

Duty is always something that you agree to. A duty is something that you do because you feel you have a moral obligation to do it. It is not something you do unwillingly, either because you fear the consequences of not doing it, or because you want to get something out of it. You do it willingly, because you feel that it is the right thing to do. For example, most people naturally feel respect for their parents, without having to be told to do so by society. In the same way, respect for the *sadguru* (true teacher) arises naturally in the aspirant.

In most cases, love of the Master can go even further than love for parents and family, when there is the understanding that the Master is indeed the Self. Love for the Self is true love that does not depend on any object. Worship of the form of the *sadguru* is therefore really worship of the Self and the acknowledgement that the Self is the only doer. Whatever spiritual practice you are engaged in, worship of the *sadguru* is your only duty, ultimately. Everything you are doing on your path is for the sake of that *sadguru*, because the *sadguru* is your own beloved Self. So there is never any question of abandoning that duty.

9.21 "Only the realized person can worship without desire." (Sri Siddharameshwar Maharaj)

Worship is an expression of devotion, which is a feeling that arises naturally. Self-realization brings the understanding that there is no one there to be realized. There is no aspirant and no Master in reality. However, the feeling of devotion that was there before realization is still there afterwards. Why would it not be? Devotion after realization has a different character in that there is no desire associated with it. There is nothing to gain. The separation that characterized the life of the aspirant has been transcended. Instead of longing, there is satisfaction and the spontaneous expression of joy. The *jnani* (realized person) rests in the Self, forgets the mind and its opposites, but continues to worship Him who is manifest in everything.

9.22 "Devotion is the mother of knowledge." (Sri Siddharameshwar Maharaj)

Devotion provides support for understanding just as a mother provides support for a child. It is a constant presence that you can always return to. Devotion to the Master opens a channel of communication, through which knowledge can be received by the mind. Because you have devotion to the Master, knowledge can remain steady. It has a focus. Without the support of devotion, knowledge tends to dissipate and becomes vulnerable to delusion.

9.23 "Devotion means faith in the Master. There is no difference between your Self and the Master's Self." (Sri Siddharameshwar Maharaj)

Devotion to the Master is devotion to the Self. The Master originally appears in the world that you take to be "outside." You meet him face-to-face. But the Master is also your own Self. You are already that Self, but you remain in ignorance of that fact. That Self will, at the appropriate time, cast off the veil of illusion that makes you believe you are living an independent life separate from It. Faith in the

Master leads directly to faith in the Self that is your own nature. You then worship the Master as Master, in the knowledge that He is your Self. There is no distinction at all.

9.24 "Divine truth which has no support of saguna worship is baseless." (Sri Siddharameshwar Maharaj)

The magic of the guru-disciple relationship comes through faith and surrender. You trust the Master enough to give up all your existing concepts, and to accept that your way of thinking has been wrong. Through that attitude of surrender, the flame of devotion in you is lit from the Master's fire. Devotion to the physical form (*saguna*) of the Master keeps the flame alight. You may have acquired some knowledge of divine truth, but how can you realize that truth, that is, become one with It, if your sense of separate identity does not go? Devotion is the means by which the walls put up by the ego are pulled down.

9.25 "Saguna worship is for the enjoyment of the devotee." (Sri Siddharameshwar Maharaj)

Worship is not for the benefit of the Master. He has nothing to gain. The act of worship is for the worshipper. It harmonizes the body, stills the mind, and allows the heart to feel peace and joy. The devotee is never apart from the Self. Worship provides a means to understand that unity. It is useful as well as enjoyable. After realization, the relationship of Master and servant remains, but it has the added beauty of the understanding of the Oneness that includes both.

9.26 "One who has both knowledge and devotion is like a king." (Sri Siddharameshwar Maharaj)

The human being is made up of body, intellect, and emotions. Satisfaction does not come from pleasing just one aspect while neglecting the others. Knowledge, by itself, can be dry. Logic alone does not produce understanding. There has to be a heart-felt desire to understand as well. In this sense, everyone on a spiritual path is a devotee.

Even Self-knowledge, though it liberates from the cycle of birth and rebirth, may not provide a full sense of joy and bliss right away. Devotion for the realized person consists in remaining in the Oneness of the Self while simultaneously worshipping the Self as all. The realized person sees that there is no difference between that Oneness and the apparent multiplicity of the world. Such a person becomes powerful, like a king, and says "everything belongs to me, because it is myself."

9.27 "In the ocean of this existence, you have the great support of devotion to the Master." (Sri Siddharameshwar Maharaj)

The teaching of Maharaj, and of Sri Siddharameshwar Maharaj and Sri Nisargadatta Maharaj, follows tradition and places great emphasis on the guru-disciple relationship, regarding it as a sacred bond through which the ancient wisdom can be transmitted. Faith in the Master and devotion to him are the vessel that can carry you across the ocean of this illusory world, which flows ceaselessly in you and around you, but which always threatens to engulf you.

It should be noted that it is not always necessary to meet the Master in physical form. Some seekers are able to form a relationship with the guru within without having to sit at the feet of another human being. However, the principles of faith and devotion are just the same for them.

The tradition of devotion to the Master and the practice of *guru-bhajana* (worshipping the guru as God) goes back a long way in Maharashtra, which is the part of India in which these Masters lived. In this tradition, God, guru, and Self, are always taken to be one and the same. In the twelfth century, Jnaneshwar praised his guru, Nivritti, in the following way:

By his mere glance,

Bondage becomes liberation,
And the knower becomes the known.

He distributes the gold of liberation to all,
Both the great and the small;
It is He who gives the vision of the Self.

As for his powers,
He surpasses even the greatness of Shiva.
He is a mirror in which the Self
Sees the reflection of its own bliss.

9.28 "In order that knowledge should remain steady, devotion is imperative." (Sri Siddharameshwar Maharaj)

In order for pure knowledge to remain pure, it is necessary to keep the ego away, because the concept "I am the doer" that is characteristic of the ego is the source of impurity. Devotion is therefore necessary so that the mind can remain clear and open. As long as you are an aspirant, faith in the Master and surrender to the divine principle that he represents are the best way to defeat the ego. Even after realization, devotion serves as nourishment for the understanding that is there, keeping the knowledge steady. Saint Tukaram writes:

Your mind has been changed;
Wrong thoughts go and He remains.
Then you understand real devotion:
Always thinking of Him and not of yourself.

9.29 "You have to worship Shiva by becoming Shiva." (Sri Siddharameshwar Maharaj)

The final result of all worship is to become one with what you are worshipping. For a long time, you think of yourself as separate from the Self, but, in the end, the illusion of separation falls away and only He remains. The "I" that you took yourself to be was the superimposition that made the illusion seem real. You then know that Oneness consciously and you do not go back into illusion. This state of complete surrender, in which the "I" does not exist, is the goal of devotion and is called *parabhakti* (beyond devotion). When that state is yours, you live in it as the Self.

9.30 "One who devotes himself to the Self, ultimately becomes the Self." (Sri Siddharameshwar Maharaj)

What is devotion about, really? What is its meaning? It may seem, at first sight, to be about offering respect to, and requesting favor from, an all-powerful being who is far above you. Some think of Him as Shiva, some as Rama, some as Lord Krishna. Others see Her as the divine mother, as Kali or Durga. In this lineage, we see Him in the form of the guru, and we bow down to Him in that form. Even though the Self may appear to the mind in many different ways, there is still only one Self, one power that appears to be two: the devotee and the object of devotion.

All the time that you lovingly worship the feet of the Master or offer fervent prayers for understanding, He is waiting, completely unconcerned, for the moment when He can reveal Himself to you. When that moment arrives, you understand that you have always been Him, and He has been you, and that you were creating the sense of separation yourself. You believed that you were ignorant, but that ignorance was an imaginary state. It is not there and never was there. In that understanding, some laugh, some cry, but all feel the relief of letting go of the burden of separate existence. Then, even though you are one with the Master, you still thank him and regard him as the greatest of all. In one of the bhajans sung in this tradition, there is this summary:

The greatness of my Master is he makes his disciples like himself.

10

October: Thinking and the Mind

10.1 "Become no mind. Don't think about anything."

Thinking is actually a phenomenon that occurs spontaneously. There are many different kinds of thoughts that arise in response to different kinds of stimuli, but they are all happening mechanically. The difficulty, or confusion, arises because of the ego. The ego is a kind of "meta-thought" that encompasses all the other thoughts. This "I-thought" gives you the sense that "you" are thinking "your" thoughts, when, in fact, nothing of the kind is happening. The ego is itself a thought. So thought is what is thinking. This is why Maharaj says "Don't think about anything." The intention is not to try to stop thinking, which is impossible, but to break the identification with the thoughts, that is, separate yourself from the thoughts. You are the thoughtless reality, which Maharaj here calls "no-mind."

10.2 "Try to understand so profoundly that your mind can't fight you."

"Your mind" is not you. You are existing at all times, with or without any mental activity going on. However, the mind, permeated with the false concept of the ego, wants to continue to *be* you, like a beggar sitting on the throne of a king. That is why understanding is emphasized over and over again. Only understanding of what you really are can restore the king to his throne. The beggar does not see things in a kingly way; many mistakes are made in governing the kingdom, but even when exposed as an impostor, he puts up a fight and doesn't want to give up his seat, because he has become accustomed to issuing orders. It is necessary to see through the ego using the Master's teaching as a light, and to understand that the ego is only a concept. When the light of profound understanding comes, the darkness of the ego is dispelled.

10.3 "Meditate on me as reality, not as the body."

When you sit and meditate on the Master, you can start by thinking of his bodily form, but the switch must be made so that you are meditating on him as the formless reality. At the same time, you let go the concept that "I" am meditating. Then you have non-duality—the formless resting in the formless. Meditation, in this sense, is essentially just silence, beingness. There are no names for it, because it is not a thing, not an object.

10.4 "Expand your thoughts and become bigger and bigger."

You need some kind of antidote for the hypnotic state brought on by habitual wrong thinking over a long period of time. There is a story about a tiger cub whose mother died and who was found and brought up by a herd of goats. The cub grew up among the young goats and assumed all of their mannerisms, eating habits, bleating, and so on. One day, a large, adult tiger came by and, examining the goat herd for a candidate for a meal, was startled to see the young tiger, now almost mature, living harmlessly among them, in a way so contradictory to its true nature. The tiger approached, the goats fled, and the young tiger was questioned. Understanding what had happened, the adult tiger took the young one to a pond where it could see its reflection clearly.

It explained that the young tiger was a tiger too and showed how the reflections of the two tigers were the same. In this way, the young tiger realized its true nature and began to roar and generally act in a manner appropriate to its birthright.

This story shows how you can make the mind bigger and bigger. As long as you take the familiar thoughts and desires to be yourself, you remain hypnotized by the thought that you are a goat. The Master's thoughts are much bigger in scope, more expansive, and more demanding. Once you accept those thoughts as your own, you can no longer forget for long what you really are.

10.5 "You must churn what the Master says. Think again and again."

For a person to sit down and actually think about an idea, with the intention of understanding what it really means, is a rare event. Generally, what is called thinking occurs mechanically and is simply a reaction to another thought. So Maharaj uses the word "churn" to indicate what is required. When milk is churned for a while, it solidifies and becomes butter. This is a symbol for the way that thinking about an idea turns into understanding. It is a similar kind of transformation. Understanding is the only way to destroy the ego.

10.6 "The mind should not be forced. Let the mind think."

There is a story about a yogi who sat to meditate. Just before he became fully absorbed in *samadhi*, a thought crossed his mind to obtain a new tiger skin to sit on, because the one he had was getting worn out. He was an adept yogi and, on this occasion, he entered into a state of *samadhi* that lasted for 2000 years. On finally returning to normal consciousness, the first thought that occurred to him was to obtain a new tiger skin. The story shows, first of all, that you should not confuse the ability to enter deep states of meditation with enlightenment, but also that the mind cannot be prevented from thinking. That is what it does and will continue to do, whether the gap between thoughts is two seconds or 2000 years.

10.7 "You become wet at once with these thoughts."

Maharaj said that we should be like the lotus leaf, that sits on the water, but does not get wet. If the leaf became wet and waterlogged, it would sink. To live in this world as a devotee or disciple of a Master, you need to keep yourself separate, as much as possible, from the false sense of identification with the I-thought. "I am doing this to get that," "I want something," and all the variations on that theme, are the thoughts that make the leaf wet, and which sink it.

10.8 "All thoughts come, good and bad, but say "It's not mine." Then you are out of it."

It seems a strange idea at first—not to think one's own thoughts— but this only indicates the depth of the habit of assuming that thoughts are real. The mind always thinks in terms of "my thoughts." But who am "I?" That it never asks. To get out of this situation, you, as an aspirant, really have no choice but to actively separate "you" from the thoughts, becoming effectively an observer of them, rather than the thinker of them. Whatever thought is arising, you say "This is not mine." This practice creates the distance necessary to begin to understand that you exist before, during, and after the arising of the thought.

10.9 "You all have the highest power in you. Welcome it. The mind must completely accept that."

What we call thoughts are called in Sanskrit *vritti*, which means "modification of the mind." Thoughts are like waves that appear on the surface of water; they modify it, but they are not different from it and have no power of their own. They come and go and the ocean remains as their source. The ocean is knowledge, which is limitless power and consciousness. What is required is that the mind, through the thoughts introduced by the Master, enquires into its own nature until it completely accepts and understands its true depth and power. Thoughts then cease to operate as though they were separate from the knowledge from which they arise, and the mind becomes pure, which Maharaj often called no-mind.

10.10 "By words I have become bound, and by words I can become free."

The human body is not born with the capacity to use words. That is a skill that is acquired through a process of trial and error during early childhood. The infant learns to objectify its sense impressions by imitating the words provided by its parents. Consciousness, which is the power that allows the process to take place, and which is the real "identity" of the child, becomes veiled by ignorance. The brain, divided into two halves, provides the basis for a mind that also divides everything into two, beginning with the fundamental duality: "I" and "not-I." This confusion of the consciousness with the I-thought creates identification with the body and is bondage.

To undo this process of misidentification, the opposite process must be applied, like unscrewing a screw or tracing a river back to its source. By enquiry into your true identity through seeking the answer to the question "Who am I?" the misunderstanding can be removed and the individual identity merged into its source. Both processes take place through the use of words and concepts.

10.11 "Mind should be made no-mind. No-mind means 'I do nothing.'"

Mind exists because you have created it and are taking it to be yourself. To put it another way, you, the subject, have projected an object called "I," and that object is now taking itself to be the subject! Where have you, the subject gone? Nowhere. You remain as the subject, but you are currently identifying with the mind, which is an object of your own creation. The mind is the apparent source of all the activity which you take to be you doing this or that. It is a phantom, not a real being.

Maharaj says that the mind should be made no-mind, which means that it should be recognized as false, as only a projection, and not the center of independent activity that it pretends to be. The mind then reverts to its original condition of pure consciousness, no-mind, or thoughtless reality.

10.12 "You must have complete conviction in the mind that nothing is true."

The ego-mind assumes that there is a world that exists independently, remaining there while it, the ego, disappears in sleep. This is ignorance. The world does not come and say "I exist." This table does not say "I'm a table." It is the mind that gives them existence. Without the mind, nothing is. If the world were true, it would laugh at you for knowing it while remaining in ignorance of yourself. So forget about the world and know what the mind is. Complete conviction that nothing is true will come when the mind itself is seen to be false.

10.13 "Right thinking is my duty."

You owe it to yourself to act in accordance with what you know to be true, even though that goes against what other people believe to be true. No one is going to force you to think rightly. You have to find the reasons to do so within yourself. To reject illusion and hold onto reality is your choice. It is important only to you. As long as you are an aspirant, you can make it your duty to apply what you have learned from the Master. If you do not do so, other people will not care. Neither will the divine power gain or lose anything. It creates and destroys millions of forms every second. It is not even aware of "you" because "you" are just thought and don't have any real existence. The illusion called "you" reaches the end of its life and then disappears. Your opportunity is wasted.

10.14 "Forget everything, forget meditation, and sit in yourself."

This statement is actually an instruction for what to do while meditating, when you reach the point where the thoughts have become quiet. Maharaj did recommend meditation to his disciples "in the beginning" and said that its purpose was to make the mind subtle. This instruction refers to the level where the mind has become subtle. You have forgotten the thoughts, including the thought "I am meditating," and are resting in pure being. This "sitting" then becomes the practice of meditation. This level of meditation generally comes after working with mantra meditation for some time.

10.15 "Mind must change, that is all."

It can hardly be emphasized often enough that the whole drama of life, the world, and spiritual search, occurs in, and through, the mind. The contents, configuration, and structure of the mind create the material from which the dream of life is projected. If you change the contents of the mind, the whole dream changes. The meaning becomes completely different. For example, what was previously felt to be true and important becomes untrue and unimportant. It is a mistake to look at the world and think it should be this way or that way, while forgetting that it comes from you. It is like the child who is trying to touch the head of its own shadow. As it reaches out to touch it, the shadow moves out of reach. The child cries until the mother comes and shows it that by touching its own head, the shadow's head is also touched. In the same way, to change the world it is necessary to change the mind.

10.16 "Think and think and finally forget everything."

The final purpose of thinking is to arrive at the understanding that there is no one who is thinking. The whole process then implodes and mind becomes one with pure knowledge or consciousness. Seeking is forgotten and peace reigns. Who is it who understands this? No one, but still understanding is there. There are no words for that thoughtless reality.

10.17 "By thinking, you can become the greatest of the greatest."

You already are the greatest of the greatest. However, to become That consciously, the mind must work at it and realize it. The way of the bird is really about thinking and the mind. It is a way that uses thinking to enquire into the nature of the mind, because once the mind is understood, everything is understood. The Master's ideas are like particles of powder poured into muddy water. As they settle, they take the impurities with them, leaving the water pure and clear so that it reflects the Self, which is shining always and everywhere.

10.18 "You have to kill your mind and say 'I don't exist. He exists in me now.'"

What is the nature of surrender? Who surrenders? If everything already belongs to the Self, surely it is presumptuous to imagine you can surrender what is not yours. Suppose there is a statue of a deity made of sugar. You break off a piece and then present it to that deity as an offering! All you can really surrender is the false concept that you are separate from Him. To give up that concept is to kill the mind. When the mind becomes no-mind ("I don't exist), the Self that always *is* becomes apparent ("He exists in me now").

10.19 "Be mute, stay in yourself, don't speak."

To abide in the Self is to rest in silent being. Silence is natural. Thinking, and the speech that is its expression, is a superimposition. It modifies the appearance of the thoughtless reality, making the world appear to exist, but it does not disturb that reality. The Self remains always unaffected, whether there are thoughts or not and whether there is speech or not. At the level of silent being, there are no individuals, no illusions. The realized person is established there, and naturally tends towards silence.

10.20 "Whenever the mind affirms 'That is true,' go against it and say 'No, it is false.'"

Nobody likes to follow a diet. When you are following a diet and the body craves chocolate or fried potatoes, you have to use will power and tell yourself "this may taste good, but it is not what I want." Following the Master's instructions is similar. You may appear to be an individual person with your own unique thoughts and desires, but actually you don't exist, only He, the divine power, exists, and this life is nothing but a long dream. The mind should put itself on a diet to adopt the Master's point of view.

Desire for understanding becomes stronger and more focused as you go on pursuing it and so you need to exert less effort rather than more. In the end, surrender to the Master is complete and you feel that everything is done for you. In the beginning, though, you have to make a habit of going against the tendency of the mind to take the world to be true.

10.21 "He gives the key. Open your mind, which is locked."

The Master gives you the key by teaching you, but you have to accept it and use it to open your mind to what he is saying. Then it will have its effect. Many seekers take the key and put it in their pocket, sometimes along with other keys they have received from other teachers, which also go unused. They never make a commitment and so all the possible doors remain locked. The Master has plenty of keys; he will give them to anyone who asks, but it is really up to the aspirant to say "I am going to use this knowledge to understand my own mind. Whatever I find along the way, I will continue until I reach the reality that the Master is speaking about." The key is free but the price of admission is your own willingness to enquire into the nature of the mind. No one else can give that to you.

10.22 "Effort is needed in the beginning. Thinking is effort."

Thinking, in the sense of churning the ideas, takes effort, just as meditation takes effort, and it is a good idea to put aside a certain time each day for it, in the same way that you put aside a time for meditation. Thinking is also like meditation in that once you have established the practice, you develop a love for it, so that you look forward to sitting down to reflect on the Master's teaching. In this sense, it ceases to become an effort, and you do it because it brings joy and so naturally you want to do it.

Whether it seems easy or difficult, you should still think and study on a regular basis, because that is the essence of this way. Understanding an idea through study is a very pleasant experience, and it brings with it the sense of achievement and progress, which is encouraging. There is nothing we cannot understand if we study.

10.23 "Guests come and go. They never become the host."

Thoughts of different qualities may come in the mind, according to the three principles of *tamas, rajas,* and *sattva.* Depressing, heavy, or negative thoughts may come. Those are *tamasic.* Thoughts about worldly goals, desires, and activities arise. Those are *rajasic.* Finally, thoughts about reality or about the spiritual path also appear. They are *sattvic* in character. These three principles are called *gunas.* They are the three aspects of *Maya,* into which the divine *shakti* (power) divides itself when it first appears.

The three types of thoughts are like the guests who come and go in a tavern. They are only passing through. They are not permanent, like the host. When the *sattvic* principle is strong, you feel the power of consciousness, of your own presence. The mind is purified and you become one with the host, which is the Self. This may occur intermittently, interrupted by periods in which *rajas* and *tamas* obscure the light of *sattvic* consciousness. With realization, all three principles are transcended and you become the host permanently.

10.24 "Nothing is yours. Be bankrupt in the mind."

To be bankrupt in the mind is to make the mind free of attachments.
A *sattvic* mind reflects reality clearly, like clear water that reflects the
sun. When you want nothing and hold on to nothing, you are free.
That is real renunciation. Even though you may have possessions
around you, if you don't identify with them or say "mine," they cannot
bind you. In fact, nothing is yours, because "you" don't exist. Only He
exists, and He is everything.

10.25 "The mind is just like a monkey, thinking of everything and then forgetting."

Because the body remains the same and we keep the same name
throughout this lifetime, it is easy to assume that there is some real
and permanent "I" occupying the body. In fact, there are innumerable
temporary "Is," each of which has its own life and its own desire. A
thought arises, lives for a few moments, and then dies. This dying is
going on constantly during the waking state; thinking and then forgetting, thinking and then forgetting, something and then nothing, something and then nothing again.

There is no fixed point in all this movement. The ego appears to be a
constant point, but it is imaginary, unreal. Where is it in deep sleep?
The ego-mind appears in the waking state and goes about its monkey-
like activities, associating from one thought to another, swinging
wildly between noble imaginings and uncouth cravings. How can this
absurd bundle of different elements possibly constitute any kind of
reality?

10.26 "Mind is your greatest friend and greatest enemy."

The mind has a very important role to play in the drama of seeking
and awakening. It changes its character during the course of the

search, transforming itself gradually from ignorance to knowledge and from darkness to light. The whole story of the Self revealing itself to the Self unfolds itself in the mind, although ultimately it is not *of* the mind. When the mind is not there, as in deep sleep, who is there to be concerned with bondage and liberation?

It is the mind that thinks and it is the mind which is capable of changing its thinking. It is the mind in which the seed of longing for reality sprouts and takes form. Thus, the mind, which in its ignorant and undisciplined state is an enemy, becomes the greatest friend, serving faithfully the cause of understanding. The mind should be like a devoted servant who puts the house in order for the absent Master. When the work is complete and the Master comes home, the servant disappears.

10.27 "As long as illusion is there, you have to think of the final reality."

When you arrive at your destination after a long journey, the concept of "destination" goes away, because you are there. You are not apart from your destination. However, as long as you are traveling, you always have to be thinking about the destination and how to get there. In the same way, the goal of reality has to be kept in mind as long as the illusion persists that you are apart from that reality. When you realize the Self, that goal disappears and you understand that you haven't gained anything you didn't already have and that you haven't gone anywhere. The destination was always under your feet.

10.28 "Tell the mind 'enough!'"

The inane and repetitious behavior of the mind can get tedious sometimes, and often one wishes one could just turn it off. However, it is in the nature of the mind to process experience and think, just as it is in the nature of the digestive system to process food and then to eliminate the waste. The problem arises when you take that spontaneous mental process to be yourself. Eventually, you may come to see that the whole of the spiritual search itself is all taking place in the mind. The mind is the seeker! Ultimately the mind's constant seeking for something becomes a burden. Then the word "enough!" comes out spontaneously as an admission of defeat and a gesture of surrender. The understanding finally comes that "I" am never going to find the solution to the problem because "I" am the problem! At that point, no doing is possible and everything is left to Him.

10.29 "Mind always thinks, but if that mind is given the understanding then the mind becomes quiet."

The main reason that the mind is full of thoughts is that there is the underlying concept of "I" as the doer of actions. As a result of this persistent notion, the mind is always thinking about how to get this thing or accomplish that thing. If the understanding comes that there is no such doer, that basis for constant thought is destroyed. The mind therefore subsides into a peaceful, quiet state. That state of deep peace that fills the mind is one of the great benefits of understanding. The mind has an inherent beauty that is not clear until its true nature as pure consciousness is revealed.

10.30 "It is not easy to cross the mind. Cross it by saying it is not true."

What is the mind? Does it have any substance, any existence of its own? If it does not, if the concept "mind" itself is not true, then there is nothing to do, nothing to cross. It becomes very simple. That is why, on this way, you enquire into the nature of the mind and understand what the mind is, so that it ceases to present a problem and is no longer an obstacle.

10.31 "The power, the effect of knowledge, must penetrate the mind. "I am the reality."

Ultimately the mind has to destroy its own ignorance. The mind is really nothing but the Self. The concept that there is some individual "thinker" is only imagination. The method by which this is revealed is Self-enquiry, in which the mind turns to focus on itself and asks "Who am I really?" Power, which is knowledge, consciousness, seeks its source and penetrates the mind. Finally, it is understood that the mind is not really there at all. Consciousness comes to the end of its search by realizing that it alone is there. Then it says with complete conviction "I am the One, I am reality."

11

November: Who Am I?

11.1 "Understand 'Who am I?' first."

It is an extraordinary fact that in this world almost no one knows who they are. Most people never think about it and simply assume that they are the body, while some, the ones who become spiritual seekers, are conscious, sometimes painfully conscious, that they do *not* know who they are. In any event, the ones who know, beyond any doubt, the answer to the question "Who am I?" are very, very few. These are the ones to go to for instruction, because, unless a person knows who he is or she is, how can they help you to know who you are?

The key problem of living is Self-ignorance, of not knowing "Who am I?" This problem can only be solved by Self-knowledge. Profound experiences and states of higher awareness will not solve the problem, because they are not incompatible with ignorance. You can have a blissful state that lasts for days or weeks, but when it goes away, you are back in the same Self-ignorance. Therefore Maharaj taught "Understand who am I first." When you know that, you know everything that needs to be known.

11.2 "Be brave enough to throw out the mind."

The mind cannot know the Self. Therefore, however essential the mind is in the earlier stages, you reach a point where you have to put your faith in that which is beyond the mind. This means surrender to Him, the Master, who is within you and also everywhere. You can't make any progress as long as you imagine that you already know who you are. You must first admit that you don't know. Throw out the mind by giving up the notion that you are someone and find what you are in reality.

11.3 "Go deep within yourself, so deep that you disappear."

"Go deep within," like "go to a higher level" is an expression that relates to the three-dimensional world that the body is familiar with. However, if you follow the instruction to "go within," you find that you go beyond the world that the body knows. If you sit quietly and close your eyes, the external, gross world fades away and you are aware of the mind only. The mind is its own world, and has its own body; the subtle body. If you continue to enquire, you find that the thoughts subside and you arrive at a state of nothingness or emptiness. This is the causal body. Going beyond it, you realize that you are still there, the one who is aware of the nothingness of the causal body. Then you simply sit in your own self-evident presence. This is the *Mahakarana* (supra-causal) body. "You" have disappeared, in that there is no individual "I" at this point, only the universal consciousness, which is aware of itself alone.

Note: This brief sketch only indicates the general direction. For a full description of the different bodies, refer to Sri Siddharameshwar's book, *Master Key to Self-Realization.*

11.4 "Nothing is mine, because I don't exist."

All the activities of the world are carried out on a wrong foundation. Human societies and human relationships, based, as they are, on the concept that there are individual persons existing everywhere, are nothing but illusions compounded. All the hatred between people and the suffering of war comes from the false identification with the body. How beautiful, how peaceful, life is when that identification is given up! It is only that identification that makes you say "mine." When you break that identification through Self-enquiry, you no longer exist as a separate person. Individual consciousness becomes universal consciousness.

11.5 "Water should understand "I'm the water, no need to drink."

When you discover that you yourself are the source of happiness, you will not seek it anywhere outside. You will not want any kind of experiences, because experiences are just temporary phenomena, while you are permanent. When you know that everything comes from you and depends on you, you will not desire external objects. Water does not need to drink because it is itself what quenches thirst. Similarly, you, the universal consciousness, do not need to seek reality because you are that reality. When you understand this, peace comes to your mind and you rest happily in yourself.

11.6 "You are the Master. You are He. Don't forget that."

You should never think that you are the body. Consciousness gives you whatever concepts you hold onto, so if you think you are the body, you will be the body. The best approach is always to think that you are He, the Master, even if you do not fully realize it yet. Then consciousness will materialize that concept instead. The trick of the Master's teaching is to put you in a position in which you can clearly see that you already have what you are looking for. The situation is like that of the man who stops reading and pushes his glasses up on top of his head. He forgets about it and starts looking for his glasses everywhere, turning the room upside-down. Even though the search is going on, there is no distance between the man and his glasses. The distance is only ignorance. Just like the man who "loses" his glasses, you already have what you are seeking. There is truly nothing to be gained in all of this so-called spirituality. It is only a matter of knowing yourself as you are, as the Self.

11.7 "You are always the truth."

Spiritual seeking can also be defined as a search for truth. Where is truth to be found? It cannot be found in the world of constantly changing forms because, however we conceive of truth, we know intuitively that it means constancy, permanence, and completeness. These are not characteristics of the ever-changing world of forms that we can see and perceive.

Just as the grains are crushed by a grindstone except the few that stick to the center pivot, truth is only to be found at the center. At the center, the grindstone is not turning and the grain is not carried away and destroyed. In this way, the mind, turning inwards and seeking its source, finds that it is itself truth; an unchanging reality that remains always stable. It remains stable because it is unmanifest, not part of the moving, changing world of manifest forms. When you know that that is what you are, you never lose that knowledge. Whatever is happening around you, you remain stable as the truth that you are.

11.8 "Finally, that emotion of the "I" thought should be absorbed."

Why does Maharaj call the "I" thought an emotion? The word "emotion" comes from the Latin "*e motus animi*," which means "from the movement of the soul." Emotion is a movement, or, if you like, a disturbance, of the inherent stillness and peace of the Self. The "I" is the fundamental movement, which is also the fundamental illusion. When the thought of "I" arises, and the Self identifies with it, the ego is there, and that is the cause of all the trouble. Therefore, that fundamental emotion should be absorbed back into its source, the Self. This is the goal of Self-enquiry.

11.9 "Thinking is not you. Who thinks? Here the thinker is not found."

Thoughts are not real. The idea that there is some real being there who is thinking the thoughts is an assumption that has no basis. When you try to find the thinker, the thinker is not found. The false assumption that there is a person is revealed as false. This is the method of Self-enquiry.

The ego cannot stand up to scrutiny. Once a man invited his son-in-law to stay at his house for the Summer. The invitation was seen by another man, an adventurer, who decided to take advantage of the situation. When the son-in-law boarded the train to go to his father-in-law's house, the adventurer got on as well. The son-in-law was greeted at the station by his brother-in-law, who had come in a car to meet him. When the son-in-law got in the car, the adventurer got in as well. The son-in-law thought that the man must be some friend of his father-in-law's family. The brother-in-law assumed that the man was a friend of the son-in-law. They reached the father-in-law's house and were all given nice rooms to stay in. At meal times, the impostor would go first and sit down and begin eating before the others and sometimes go into the kitchen and demand certain kinds of food that he liked. The father-in-law noticed this bad behavior, but didn't say anything because he did not want to hurt the feelings of this person, who, he assumed, must be an intimate friend of his son-in-law. The impostor would also go into the son-in-law's room and borrow his clothes without asking. Although the son-in-law was annoyed by this, he didn't complain because he took the man to be a member of his father-in-law's household.

This went on for some time and the impostor was enjoying himself immensely. Eventually the father-in-law became so fed up that he went to the son-in-law and asked him directly why he had brought such a man with him. At the same time, the son-in-law wanted to ask the father-in-law who is this nuisance who puts on all my clean shirts and soils them? The impostor found out that father-in-law and son-in-law were making enquiries about him and slipped away by the back door. The ego is just this kind of impostor, an unwelcome guest who is allowed to do what he likes only through the ignorance of the host.

11.10 "You are never lost. Then why do anything to find yourself?"

Even if you say "I am lost," the one who is saying "I am lost" is the Self, which can never be lost. So the concept of being lost, and of needing to find yourself, is in the mind. It is only a wrong conclusion. The situation is often illustrated by the story of the tenth man.

Ten men crossed a river. When they reached the other side, the leader decided to count their number to make sure that all had crossed safely. He counted his comrades but forgot about himself and so, to his dismay, concluded that one man had been lost on the way across. Each one counted, but each made the same error. Then they all sat down and wept at their loss. Presently, a wise man came by and asked them what was the matter. On hearing the explanation, he realized immediately what had happened and proposed to show them that they had no need for sorrow. He stood them in a row and made each one call out his number. When he got to the last man, he tapped him on the chest. When the last man was tapped, he realized he was the tenth man. Repeating the procedure for each man, the wise man showed them that they had not lost anyone and they all went happily on their way. The practice of spiritual seeking is based on a similar error. The Self is always present but it is not known, not realized.

11.11 "You never forget yourself. You are always there. But you misinterpret the 'I.'"

It is very important to understand that you are always there. There is never any time that you can say "I am not." Your existence is your most intimate, most familiar experience. You never forget yourself. You are always there. The Self that you are is Self-shining. It does not require any other light to illuminate it and so you do not require any-one else to tell you that you are. However, as long as you misinterpret the "I," identifying yourself with the body, you cannot experience the Self in its natural fullness and completeness. Instead, you feel a sense of lack, of incompleteness. The solution to this misinterpretation is discrimination. Enquire into who you are and discard one by one the different bodies that are not you.

A man went to a holy man and asked to be introduced to God. The holy man said "When I go to Him, He will ask about you. What can I tell Him? Show me your credentials." The man pointed to his body and spoke his name. The holy man replied "These are temporary and superficial attributes. They are not you. Show me your real credentials." The man then thought that perhaps his thoughts, desires, and feelings were his real credentials. "These are also temporary and fleeting forms. They are not you. Show me your true, permanent credentials." In this way, the man was brought to see his real nature beyond forms and, after that, he did not ask for any more introductions.

11.12 "Body is not Self, mind is not Self, knowledge is not Self. Final reality is Self."

When you first hear about universal consciousness and final reality, they may seem far away, remote from where you are, and consequently the feeling arises that you have to attain them. This feeling arises because you take yourself to be the body and the mind. In fact, you are sitting in final reality, the pure knowledge or consciousness is your beingness, and the mind and body are objects of your awareness. An analogy is that of the sun. You are the sun, consciousness or knowledge is your radiance, and the subtle and gross bodies are the worlds that you give life to.

11.13 "In final reality, there is no you, no I, no mind, no thought. That is your state."

You, as final reality, do not know your own knowledge, you are not aware of it, and so, in deep sleep, you are there, but you are not conscious of the worlds of mind and body. Knowledge only appears in the waking and dream states. It is impermanent. The concepts of "I" and "you" appear in these states only. When the ego is destroyed, the "I" does not remain as the false concept of a separate individual but only as the "I am," which is pure knowledge or universal consciousness.

This "I amness" is the highest experience, it is God, *Ishwara, sat-chit-ananda*—it has many names. However, your knowing yourself as That depends on this current, bodily form for its experience. "I am" is dependent on the food consumed by a body to experience itself. This experience, in a particular form, has a limited lifespan. Therefore, you cannot take it to be the final reality, but as the manifest aspect of reality. Your radiance is giving life to everything, you are playing everywhere as consciousness, but still you remain as final reality, unaffected by the creation of the worlds.

11.14 "First you must know yourself, and then you go a little ahead and then forget yourself."

Imagine that you are a doll made out of salt and that you fall into the ocean. At first you retain your form, but then gradually you begin to dissolve until finally you don't exist at all anymore—you have become one with the ocean of salt-water. Self-knowledge or Self-realization can be compared to the salt doll falling in the ocean. It occurs suddenly, with a splash, although from another point of view it is only the last of a long sequence of moments, just as the doll splashing into the ocean is only the culmination of a process of falling through the air. Natural processes are like that: a sequence of development in a certain direction, followed by a sudden change of state.

When you get knowledge of the Self, you think "I am one with Brahman," "I am what I was seeking," "I am He," and so on. You rejoice in your new state and enjoy the new sense of freedom that comes with it. Then, after a while, the state settles down and you cease to say "I am *Brahman*, I am He." Instead, you simply live as that formless reality, without effort. You forget yourself as you become more and more dissolved. Sri Siddharameshwar Maharaj compared it to a man coming out of the blazing sun into the welcoming shade of a large tree. At first, he says "Aah! Aah!" with relief, but then, after a while, he lays still and just rests in the cool depth of the shade.

11.15 "Your innermost feeling required is I am He and nothing else."

The world of the mind is an illusion. All of the concepts that arise are untrue. That is why it is said that in reality there is nothing to understand. Understanding itself is ultimately false, because it is based on concepts. Likewise, here, Maharaj says that the innermost "feeling" required is that I am He. This is different from the thinking "I am He" that goes on in the beginning of practice. That is all very useful at a certain stage, but later you have to become completely convinced of the fact that you are He, the reality.

When ignorance goes, conviction is a feeling or emotion that is always there. You don't need to think about it. Just as now, if someone asks you if you are a human being, you don't have to think about it, you just know it, you feel it in every part of your body. In the same way, when there is conviction, you know beyond any doubt that you are He.

11.16 "You have forgotten Him. Reality is yourself. You have forgotten yourself."

One has to be very careful with the concepts of remembering and forgetting, because the ego-mind will quickly interpret them in the wrong way. As soon as it hears the idea "you have forgotten yourself" it will start to try to remember itself. In so doing, it strengthens its own central position. Remembering has to be practiced in a spirit of surrender, in the understanding that what you are remembering is not the ego-mind, but the reality that is beyond the mind.

The mind trying to remember itself is like a character in a dream murmuring to itself "I must remember who I am." It remains within the dream. The solution is to understand that this really is all a dream, and that "I," being reality itself, am not in the dream at all. "I have forgotten myself because I have taken the dream to be true, I have identified myself with that dream character." When this understanding comes, the dream may continue, but how can it affect you?

11.17 "Happiness is yourself. Does water get thirsty?"

Happiness is not something that can be gained by anybody. That is the mistake that keeps the human being trapped in its restless cycle of desire, fulfillment, and disillusion. You cannot find happiness anywhere because happiness is yourself. You are That. To seek it outside is to look in totally the wrong direction and can only lead to frustration. Eventually, this understanding comes to many people and they become seekers, looking within for fulfillment. This is an improvement, even though the search does not end at that point. Happiness, contentment, peace, and joy are flowing like a fountain in your own heart. They are your very nature. Therefore, seek only to know your true nature. Find out "Who am I?"

11.18 "The presence of the Self is the only happiness."

Is the Self present at some times and absent at others? No, it is always there, and that is why, in our heart of hearts, we always feel that happiness is natural for us and that unhappiness or suffering is unnatural. People generally tend to be hopeful, resilient, adaptable, always living in hope of future happiness, even if it is denied to them today.

The problem lies in the confused ideas we have about the source of happiness. Few people understand that happiness comes from the Self. Consequently, they look for it in external objects. They do not know that even the fleeting happiness that comes through the fulfilment of some desire, such as when a desirable object is finally acquired, comes from the presence of the Self, when the Self is resting in itself after being released from the burden of the desire. True, or permanent, happiness comes when we get rid of the greater burden of ignorance, of imagining that we are not happiness already, and of imagining that we are limited individuals who are compelled to seek happiness.

11.19 "Find out yourself. You are not found anywhere, but still you are there."

The world is not true. It is an appearance and its only substance is the Self. Through the inscrutable power of its *Maya*, the Self, while remaining unmanifest, makes the universe manifest. Where are "you" in this scheme of things? Are you part of the fleeting manifestation or are you part of the unmanifest source? Are you both? Or neither? You must find out. If you do not know who you are, what is the meaning of this so-called life?

Maharaj gives two pointers here. First of all, "You are not found anywhere." This means that everything you have taken yourself to be is wrong. You are not the body, not the mind, not thoughts or the absence of thoughts, not perceptions or sensations. You are not even the knowledge of your own existence, which is absent in sleep. All of these things are of the nature of a dream. They appear. How long do they last?

Secondly, "Still you are there." You will know yourself when you put aside all the things listed above. You are still there, yes, but what can be said about that condition? There are no words, no concepts that remain to describe it. It has to be realized directly.

11.20 "Space can be perceived and felt, reality cannot, so forget that space and you are He, always."

Reality cannot be perceived or felt, because perceiving and feeling are functions that operate in the dream realm and reality is not in that dream. Nothing in the dream world can experience the deep sleep of the dreamer. The subject cannot be objectified. You cannot see your own eyes. However, when you realize your Self, you know who you are, and you don't need any confirmation. You are Self-shining even now, only ignorance stands in your way. Ignorance is like space, it can be perceived and felt—you can be aware of it—but it is not really there. Self-ignorance and Self-forgetfulness are the same. What you need to do is forget the forgetfulness, forget the space, which means to become aware of yourself as reality, existing permanently beyond the space of forgetfulness.

11.21 "I don't exist. In this way, all actions in the moment are actionless."

Actionless means that there is no doer. Actions happen but they take place in a dream, without anyone deciding whether they should happen one way or another. If you take a minute to look back on the things that have happened to you during the day, or during the day yesterday, you will see a series of images, in which the body is walking or standing or sitting. The body appears as an object. These scenes change, but consciousness remains still and unchanging. The body moves but the Self does not move. It is as though wherever the body went, consciousness was already there. This is how actions appear when there is the understanding "I don't exist." The doer of the actions is nowhere to be found.

11.22 "Knowingness lasts up till the last moment."

The nature of embodiment is knowingness. Knowledge is the medium of perception and the fundamental perception is the knowledge of one's own existence, the knowledge "I am." All other perceptions, and the whole experience of the world, sprouts from this seed. Even in deep sleep, knowingness remains in a dormant state. Then, when we enter the waking state, we say "I slept well." How do we know that? Because knowingness was there. Therefore, knowingness lasts throughout the life, sometimes appearing in the form of sleep, sometimes as dream during sleep, and sometimes as the dream that we call the waking state. Knowingness is the essence of the food taken in by the body. It cannot exist without that food, just as a flame cannot exist without fuel, and so, when the body dies, the flame of knowingness persists for a little while and then goes out.

11.23 "The seed of birth and death is the subtle body, which is of the nature of desire." (Sri Siddharameshwar Maharaj)

Note: The remaining quotations in this chapter are from Sri Siddharameshwar Maharaj.

Birth and death are in the subtle body, that is, they are only concepts that appear in the mind. The seed from which births sprout is the consciousness "I am," which contains within it the desire to be. It is the nature of consciousness to create the birth of a form, to sustain it through the desire to be, and then to destroy it. No one can say why this is so. Scriptures can only say that it is the play of consciousness, or God's *lila*.

Once consciousness has taken a form, the desire to be (or to become), makes the form seek experiences, thus causing actions. Further actions take place as a consequence of previous actions, creating a tapestry of cause and effect that connects all forms in an infinitely complex pattern. This universe of forms is thus a perfectly self-regulating system in which everything happens in the only way it can happen. There are no individuals anywhere. The concept of being an individual arises in the human mind through the identification of the consciousness with the bodily form that happens to be there.

11.24 "The causal body is a state of pure forgetfulness." (Sri Siddharameshwar Maharaj)

When you meditate using the mantra, you may come after a while to a peaceful state in which the thoughts have stopped and breathing is light or even unnoticable. That is the state of the causal body. It is really a state of forgetfulness of thoughts, the state of zero from which thoughts arise and into which they dissolve. It is a relatively good state in that it is closer to reality than the subtle body, which is the world of thoughts.

The causal body is experienced as peaceful because it is not subject to the disturbance of constant thinking. However, it should not be taken for reality. Ignorance remains in the causal body. You have still forgotten who you are. It is only when you realize that you are there as the self-shining presence that is aware of the forgetfulness of the causal body that you become that Self. Then you go beyond zero and beyond forgetfulness.

11.25 "By reason of forgetfulness each human being feels he is ignorant and struggles to obtain knowledge." (Sri Siddharameshwar Maharaj)

What is the nature of this forgetfulness that makes each person feel that he or she is ignorant? Is that forgetfulness really anything but ignorance itself? The causal body, which is really pure ignorance or forgetfulness, lies like an impenetrable veil between the mind (the subtle body) and Self-knowledge (the *Mahakarana* or supra-causal body). The causal body is the cause of that Self-ignorance that lasts as long as you do not know who you really are. That ignorance is sometimes described as a veil, or as darkness, or as clouds obscuring the sun. In all cases: ignorance and knowledge, darkness and light, forgetting and remembering, there is a duality involved, which means that you are dealing with an interpretation of the mind. Reality is beyond duality.

Knowledge, light, and remembering are all indications of the condition of the mind that is considered desirable, the positive half of the balance. Ignorance, darkness, and forgetfulness are indications of the condition that is considered undesirable in the mind of the spiritual seeker, and which represent the negative side. These pairs of opposites provide a way of thinking that is useful in the beginning. However, they cannot penetrate the veil of ignorance because they are in the mind and are therefore "below" it. The only way to cross that gap of the causal body is to enter it by leaving the mind behind. This is why meditation is such a useful aid. Through meditation, you can forget the mind and experience the sensation of entering the more rarefied atmosphere of the causal body. You enter a state of pure forgetfulness. Ultimately, you forget that forgetfulness and realize your true existence beyond both remembering and forgetting.

11.26 "The state of forgetfulness is really non-existent." (Sri Siddharameshwar Maharaj)

It is truly wonderful and liberating to understand that ignorance does not exist! From a purely logical point of view, it is clear that what is not there cannot *be*. Ignorance, forgetfulness, is an absence, a state of non-being. Such a state cannot be experienced. How can you ever experience your own non-existence? It is impossible! Therefore the causal body, that state of pure ignorance that is taken, for the sake of explanation, to be the obstacle to Self-knowledge, is not really there. It isn't any thing. There's no thing there! This is why it is said over and over again that the whole process of spiritual seeking, of bondage and liberation, of ignorance and knowledge, takes place in the mind. Ignorance is an imaginary state. You only imagine that you are not realized, not enlightened. Actually, that enlightenment is your natural state right now. The whole search ends with the understanding that you were imagining your own ignorance.

11.27 "The Mahakarana body can be experienced as pure knowledge." (Sri Siddharameshwar Maharaj)

The *Mahakarana* body *is* pure knowledge and so, when it is experienced, pure knowledge is knowing itself. What is that experience like? There is still the sense of individual "I" in the mind, because mind *is* the sense of individual "I." That sense does not go away, but at the same time there is the understanding that one's real existence is a light that is shining beyond the mind. The experience of pure knowledge is a self-contained presence. Just as the sun does not require any other light to see itself because it *is* light, so pure consciousness does not require any other consciousness to know itself because it *is* knowledge.

11.28 "The state of awareness in the Mahakarana body is the self-lit flame which makes itself bare after making the ignorance forget itself." (Sri Siddharameshwar Maharaj)

This statement is a description of how Self-realization takes place through enquiry into the nature of the "I." If you consistently contemplate the causal body in your meditation, you will come to the point where you realize that the real "I" is yourself, the one who is aware of that forgetfulness. You are real and the ignorance that you were contemplating is not real. It was always like that; you were always there, but you did not realize it, because you believed in the reality of ignorance. Your state of awareness then becomes permanent—the self-lit flame. Forgetting that you *are* becomes impossible. At that point you have done everything that needs to be done, or rather, it has been done through you. The Self has realized itself.

11.29 "Whatever is remembered or forgotten is definitely not you." (Sri Siddharameshwar Maharaj)

Remembering and forgetting are two opposites that make up the worlds of the subtle body and the causal body, respectively. Thoughts have to be "forgotten" before they can be remembered. They come from ignorance and return to it, like actors appearing from the wings of the stage, speaking their lines and then retiring. That is the nature of the perceived world; it is seen and then it is not seen. None of this can be you. Your permanence and reality is of a totally different order to these fleeting and ephemeral phenomena. If you had to remember something in order to exist, you would be dependent on that which you are remembering. Then where would "you" be when you had forgotten it? Reality cannot come and go like that. The Self is independent. Worlds may come and go but the Self remains as it is.

11.30 "These four bodies are the four steps to go on to the fifth rung, where word becomes silent." (Sri Siddharameshwar Maharaj)

In the final analysis, the four bodies: gross, subtle, causal, and *Mahakarana* or supra-causal, are all part of manifestation. Everything in this manifestation is mechanical. It operates by itself, like a vast, perfectly oiled machine, or, if you prefer an organic simile, like a great tree growing from a single seed. The gross and subtle bodies are the form and the name of the created objects, the causal body is the nothingness from which they appear, and the *Mahakarana* body is the radiant and divine power that gives life to everything.

Only the unmanifest is beyond all this. What can be said about that which does not appear or disappear, which is beyond existence and non-existence? Word becomes silent there. In reality, there is no possibility of thinking or conceptualizing. When there is only One, how can anything appear? Appearance, manifestation, means duality: one to see and one to be seen. And yet that "there" is also "here." The final reality, where words cannot reach, is the eternal foundation for this moment, this experience. That stateless state has no divisions, parts, interruptions, modifications, or characteristics of any kind. That is what we are, now and forever.

12

December: The Realized Person

12.1 "The body has no free will. Free will is always for the realized person."

Free will is a concept that is considered almost sacred in the West, but which has no foundation in reality. It simply does not correspond to the way things are and, sooner or later, it has to be abandoned in favor of surrender to a higher power. The "free will" that the realized person enjoys comes from complete surrender. To see and experience the perfection of things as they are and to accept without reservation is true freedom of the will. The realized person always has the attitude "Thy will be done."

As an aspirant, however, you cannot simply say "thy will be done" and stop making any effort. To go that way is to misunderstand Advaita. This mistake is illustrated by the story of the man who stood in the way of the elephant. The elephant's handler called out to the man to move but the man just said "I am God, the elephant is God, everything is God's will." Of course, he was knocked down and injured by the elephant. When he complained to his guru, saying that he had only repeated what the guru had told him, the guru said "the elephant's handler, who told you to get out of the way, was also God, but you chose to ignore Him at that point."

12.2 "Realized persons understand by mind only."

The real, or final, understanding, is that there is no one who has anything to gain, no one who is seeking, and no one to understand. This understanding is what the apparent journey of spiritual seeking is heading towards. It should be clear, though, that the mind itself meets its death in this realization (which is why it is called "final" understanding). Unwittingly, the ego-mind brings about its own death. The ideas of the Master, once accepted and absorbed, transform the mind completely, reducing it to its original state of no-mind, or pure consciousness. Realization is the last scene of the last act for the purified mind. The curtain comes down on the false "doer." There is no repeat performance.

12.3 "The realized person says 'I'm never right, I'm always wrong.'"

The phrase "realized person" is only used for the purposes of communication, to indicate that there is a fundamental change that occurs, and which is called realization or enlightenment. In fact, there is no "person" to be realized. Realization is really the understanding that the concept of individual existence as a "person" was an illusion, a mistake, a misinterpretation. The so-called realized person knows this very well and so he or she says "I'm never right, I'm always wrong." After realization, you may answer when someone calls your name and may continue to act in the world, but you will never take yourself to be an individual entity, separate from your source as pure consciousness.

12.4 "The realized man's wish is always fulfilled. He wants reality. So he is never unhappy, he is always happy."

The paradox of spiritual seeking is that you have no free will but at the same time you have to act as though everything depends on your own choices and your own efforts. This is the humor of the situation from the "divine" point of view. What you want is what you get. Seek and you shall find. This is right and appropriate and you should persist until you know that you have got what you want and found what you were seeking. Then you are out of the circle of ignorance.

The realized person has got out of the circle of ignorance and into a "circle of happiness." If the question arises "What do I want?" the answer comes "I want only reality, the Self." Then it is immediately understood that I already am that reality. In that understanding there is happiness and fulfilment. Consequently, there is no need, and no room, for any other desire.

12.5 "When you understand, then the power is there and everything you do is 'correct.'"

After final understanding, you find that you understand whatever you need to understand. Ideas which were previously unclear become clear as daylight to you. That understanding is like a power that is manifest in you. You feel in harmony, in tune with your surroundings. You feel that what is happening is right, and could not be otherwise. Because you feel this power in you and around you, your actions are also "correct." You find yourself without goals or ambitions, but still, that which needs to be done, is done. Like a person travelling by train, you know that the train is going somewhere and is carrying you; you don't have to do anything. You put your bag in the rack. You don't carry it on your back any longer.

12.6 "If you understand that 'nothing cannot touch me,' then you are a realized person."

To say that the world is nothing is not to belittle it or make light of the sufferings that others are experiencing. All that is as it is. You cannot change it. However, for you, when final understanding is there, the world is as nothing. It doesn't disappear, your wordly troubles don't go away, and you do not become suddenly a better person. Nevertheless, you understand at the deepest, most intuitive level that it is all nothing and it cannot touch you in any way. It is not really possible to describe this in words.

What seems to happen with final understanding is that you become established in a sense of reality that is absolutely fundamental, as though you were existing as an unmoving center, around which everything was turning, coming into being, and moving out of being again. Because you always know yourself as this unchanging, true center, you automatically have the knowledge that what you perceive is not true, because, as perception, it is *other* than that center. On the other hand, because you always experience that true center, you do not experience your perceptions as false. You are always experiencing reality, even while you are perceiving something, and so perception is also an experience of reality for you.

12.7 "When you know everyone is myself, then what you do, it's all the same to you."

After realization, you find that you don't mind how things go, whether you do one thing or some other thing. Why do you feel such indifference? Because you know that all that activity doesn't really have anything to do with you. It is all happening according to the *prarabdha karma*, that is, according to those tendencies which have already been set in motion and which must come to fruition through the body and mind. This karma is like the arrow which has already been released from the bow. It cannot be stopped or turned back in its flight. That is your external life after realization. There is nothing for you to do. Similarly, when you know everyone is yourself, you don't crave the company of particular people. You get on perfectly well with anyone and you are inclined to treat everyone with the same respect.

12.8 "Try to understand the realized person, what they say. They say they have never done anything in their life."

To imagine that realization is a state of great personal power is wrong. Realization is the essence of impersonality. In the realized person, the concept of the individual has been effaced. It is fully understood that the notion of being a person was an illusion. You know that it is an illusion, even though that notion is the whole basis for society, culture, philosophy, psychology, and so on. This understanding is so completely radical that very few people can even hear it without rejecting it outright. Of those few, still fewer will actually accept the truth of it.

The acceptance and understanding that there never has been any "doer" is one of the characteristics of the realized person. He or she knows that everything that has happened, from birth in a particular body, through the beginning of spiritual seeking, to the final understanding, has all happened without the intervention of any individual, and that the concept of the individual itself was only a wrong assumption.

The realized person may be very reluctant to use the word "I," because it is understood that there is no "I" in the sense in which it is usually taken. He or she may therefore attempt to speak without it, perhaps using a phrase such as "this one" instead of using the personal pronoun, or may speak in a passive voice, using phrases such as "realization has occurred," instead of "I have realized." Realization is understood to be the Self realizing itself, through itself. The realized person will generally never say "I am a realized person," because it simply doesn't make any sense. Realization happens, but it does not happen to an "I."

12.9 "I am never bored. Why? Because I don't think."

It is not usually understood that boredom comes from thinking and leads to a negative emotion. As soon as the thought comes "I have nothing to do, I'm bored," the mind becomes restless and unhappy, and the body starts looking for something to occupy its attention. The more affluent the society, the more emphasis there is on finding novel ways to stave off the malaise of boredom. People are bombarded with advertisements and tantalized with suggestions for further consumption, all of which have the effect, intentional or otherwise, of making the mind think "oh, if I only had that/was there/could do that, I wouldn't be so bored."

The realized person, on the other hand, does not think about anything. Who thinks? Thoughts may occur when they are appropriate (or even when they are not appropriate!) but what effect can they have if no one claims them? The enlightened one does not crave this rather than that and so does not indulge in desire nor experience the thoughts that follow in the train of desire.

12.10 "This Paramatman in the form of Brahman will likewise remain happy whatever the situation." (Sri Siddharameshwar Maharaj)

Note: The remaining quotations in this chapter are from Sri Siddharameshwar Maharaj.

Paramatman is the final reality. It exists in itself but does not know itself. To know itself, it must manifest. Reality manifests itself as the power of *Brahman*, or pure consciousness, taking innumerable forms through age after age. None of the forms, however, result in any diminution or change in the reality itself. It is the creating and veiling power of *Brahman*, called *Maya*, that causes that pure consciousness to identify itself with the form. In this way, reality gets itself involved with the life of the forms, the world of manifestation, and forgets itself as reality.

From time to time, however, that same consciousness remembers and realizes itself, knowing once again that it is the supreme reality, existing in itself, untouched by the created world, which it now sees as insubstantial, fleeting, amounting to zero. This understanding, or Self-knowledge, means that the pure consciousness remains as happiness, because happiness (*ananda*) is its nature. This remains the case, whatever the situation of the form in which this realization has occurred. The form in which this Self-knowledge has arisen is called a realized person.

12.11 "That body which has the knowledge of the Self in it will perforce emit light." (Sri Siddharameshwar Maharaj)

What is light and how can it be emitted from one body and not from another? You have probably had the experience at some time of being in a particularly high state of consciousness, in which you felt your own reality beyond any doubt. Perhaps you felt completely centered in the Self or felt a state of bliss without cause. In any of these circumstances, your body is emitting light. As it says in the Bible:

When the eye is single, the whole body is filled with light. (Luke 11:34)

Usually, this light is not emitted, because it is absorbed by ignorance, doubts, and ego-centered thinking. When these obstructions are removed, the light of consciousness and understanding naturally shines and can be perceived by others as a sense of peace and joy.

12.12 "To see everyone as part of the one reality is the characteristic of such a jnani." (Sri Siddharameshwar Maharaj)

There was a man who built a room full of mirrors. He put them on the ceiling, on the walls, and at all angles. He loved to go in the room and see his reflection everywhere. One day, he left the door to this room open and his dog went inside. Immediately it saw what it imagined to be dozens of other dogs all around it. It started running at them, barking and fighting, becoming more and more exhausted until finally it fell down and died.

It is the nature of the divine sight to see all beings as parts of the same reality, and so the *jnani* (realized person) thinks "Everyone is myself. I see myself everywhere I look." The ego, on the other hand, is like the dog. It sees others as separate and as potentially hostile. The sense of separation creates fear, which leads to aggression. There is no peace for the ego, or for a world in which the ego is dominant.

12.13 "After one meets oneself, the body is realized to be untrue." (Sri Siddharameshwar Maharaj)

To meet yourself is to know yourself, finally, and to know yourself means to know what you are not. You are not any particular form. You are not the body that you happened to identify with. All forms appear in you as a continuous stream: thoughts, feelings, sense perceptions of all kinds, movement and the absence of movement. Your experience of the body is not an experience of a single "thing" but a flow of these various perceptions, all of which happen in your awareness. This is how you see the body after understanding and it makes you free of it.

12.14 "For the realized one, it is all One. There is no duality." (Sri Siddharameshwar Maharaj)

Many seekers have their own ideas about what it means to be realized. But what does realization really mean? In the first place, there is no duality for such a person. All is One. Again, some people imagine that Oneness means a kind of permanent mystical vision, in which one can automatically penetrate into the essence of things, read minds, see other peoples' past lives, and so on.

The reality is much simpler and more prosaic. To be realized is natural, normal. It is the ego that is unnatural and abnormal. Therefore, when realization occurs, the one to whom it happens simply reverts to the normal condition. The sense of being a separate individual is replaced with the sense of simple being. The key fact of realization is its simplicity. It is really "nothing special." There is nothing more ordinary and obvious than reality. That is exactly why it is overlooked. Often, people are seeking something that they imagine to be extraordinary—some shattering revelation or profound awakening that is somehow prolonged indefinitely. But all such concepts are in the realm of duality, while reality is not. How then can reality be known through concepts? Everything that people imagine Oneness to be is wrong. Oneness is simply what is, as it is.

12.15 "The liberated one just stops worrying about this mundane life. Outwardly and inwardly, there is complete, unshakable contentment." (Sri Siddharameshwar Maharaj)

When He, the Master, makes you He, who is there left to be concerned about anything? There is literally nothing to worry about. For a realized person to worry, he or she would have to re-adopt a whole series of false assumptions and then re-believe in them. Of course, that will not happen. Therefore, there is an absence of any kind of worry, from the most trivial anxiety to the fear of death. There is contentment that is experienced as being itself. The Self has realized itself and simply lives as pure awareness.

Why does the Self realize itself? Does It realize itself to continue to live as a seeker, as a small creature, as a devotee in awe of the great mystery of reality? No! It realizes itself to live this life as the Self, as God. The Lord ascends His throne and enjoys this world as His own creation. It is only the enjoyment of the moment that is real and alive. The liberated one is aware of what is, but is not concerned, knowing that the Divine Power is making things happen in the only way that they can happen.

12.16 "Just to listen, contemplate, meditate, these are the signs of a realized one." (Sri Siddharameshwar Maharaj)

After all doubts are gone and you understand that you are He, what is there left to do? "You" no longer exist as a center of volition and so action becomes actionless. Living becomes non-volitional. Desires may arise according to the *prarabdha karma*, that is, the tendencies that still have to come to fruition, but you know yourself to be beyond that. As long as the body lasts, you remain as its witness. Listening, contemplating, meditating arise naturally. You are satisfied to take a back seat and watch God's creation play itself out.

12.17 "Once the Self is known, there is no restriction on your action," (Sri Siddharameshwar Maharaj)

The concept of bondage implies restrictions, limitations. What is the nature of that bondage? It is that you take yourself to be something that you are not. You are bound by your identification with the body-mind. Liberation means that that identification is broken and you remain what you always were in reality. There is no restriction, no artificial limitation created by the mind's imaginings. Now you are free to be your Self which you always were, but did not know it.

The ego thinks "after realization, there are no restrictions, so I can do exactly what I like." The ego always thinks in this way. How can it understand that it is itself the restriction that is removed by liberation? So when Sri Siddharameshwar Maharaj says that there is no restriction on your action, he means that you are free from the burden of self-centered desire, resistance to what is, and non-acceptance. These are the real restrictions and limitations that prevent you from enjoying the beauty and simplicity of pure being.

12.18 "A realized person knows that the Self is the only truth and that all the rest is just a play of thoughts." (Sri Siddharameshwar Maharaj)

To be firm and secure in reality, it is necessary to know the Self as the truth and everything else as untrue. The truth is overlooked because it is so simple, so obvious. Many people are expecting something else. When you see the truth in all its simplicity, you may be astonished that it is so easy. It is like the experience of a man who, when he gets off a train after a long journey, which he spent in some anxiety because he had no ticket, looks around for someone to pay. He's amazed that there's no one to pay, no one to thank. There's no charge. The journey was free! Now he knows he can get on any train and go anywhere without restriction.

12.19 "The sign of true spiritual knowledge is that one is free of all doubts." (Sri Siddharameshwar Maharaj)

A doubt means that you are not certain that something is true. For example, the doubt may persist "How can I be He, the reality?" There is a nagging feeling that in fact it may *not* be true. Even the faith that one has in the Master may not be enough to completely dispel that doubt and silence it forever. As long as there are doubts, there is ignorance, because doubts and ignorance are essentially the same thing. This is why Sri Siddharameshwar Maharaj says here that it is a sign of true understanding that there are no doubts at all. Realization means the destruction of ignorance. Afterwards, there is no possibility of doubt arising. The source of doubt, which is the false thought of separate existence as ego, has been uprooted. It no longer interposes itself, asking useless questions, and wondering "can it really be true?" There is only clear seeing, unimpeded by any doubt.

12.20 "Abide in your being or Self-nature." (Sri Siddharameshwar Maharaj)

There is no need for any kind of study after Self-realization. The spiritual books that you struggled to understand when you were a seeker no longer have anything to teach you. Before enlightenment, you couldn't properly understand them, and, after enlightenment, they are of no use!

You don't have to say to yourself "I am He, I am the Self," because you just know. Your being is your knowing. You have no further use for "spirituality." One who has come to the end of the journey no longer needs the map or the directions for how to get there. Even so, you cannot simply let your mind drift and wander wherever it wants, like a bad servant. As long as the body is there, the mind should remain steady in the contemplation of its revealed being.

12.21 "Even realized ones can, on abandonment of the Self, become bewildered." (Sri Siddharameshwar Maharaj)

One of the laws that operate in the Universe is the law of entropy. This law states that every closed system tends to greater and greater disorder. Applying this principle to the mind, it means that whenever there is no discipline, the mind descends into more and more random patterns of association. Simply put, it means that if you don't keep your mind focused, you will become confused.

This law still applies to the mind after realization. Whether one is an aspirant or a Master, one has to remain vigilant. Sri Neem Karoli Baba said:

The eyes of a saint are always concentrated on the supreme Self. The minute he is aware of himself, sainthood is lost.

12.22 "To be with one's own nature is the main requisite of a realized person." (Sri Siddharameshwar Maharaj)

For an aspirant, the realized person is useful because he or she is a living example of the Self. So are you, but you do not know it with conviction. The realized person is one with his or her own true nature. When you sit in their presence, you can experience your own nature. This happens, not because of anything they are doing, but simply because it is a universal law that like attracts like. You are actually experiencing the One true nature; it does not belong to the aspirant or to the Master, but it is apparent in the presence of one who lives as That. This simple being in silence is the main thing that the realized person "does." Any verbal teaching comes out of that pure silence.

12.23 "All this chaos is the chaos of illusion. Let the objects be whatever they are." (Sri Siddharameshwar Maharaj)

Why should one who understands and realizes the oneness of the Self meddle in the world of illusory forms? Sometimes there is some *karma* that causes the realized person to take a very visible and active role: perform miracles, found religions, or become widely known in some other way. These cases amount to what is probably a small minority of the enlightened in this world. Realization means understanding that there is no doer for all the actions that are done. This understanding does not encourage an active, goal-oriented life, but tends to support a passive, contemplative existence, one that leaves the objects of the world as they are.

12.24 "Doership rests in Maya and non-doership in Brahman." (Sri Siddharameshwar Maharaj)

From the point of view of the ego, the realized person may seem unmotivated, even lazy. This is actually a more or less correct perception, as far as it goes. In the *Ashtavakra Gita*, it says:

Who is lazier than the Master? He has trouble even blinking!

What this means is that the enlightened person understands that whatever appears to be done in the world, he or she is in fact not doing anything. It is all *Maya*, the illusion of ignorance.

Sri Siddharameshwar Maharaj tells a story about a princess who decides she wants to marry a truly lazy man. The notice goes out and from all over the kingdom prospective suitors come. Some demonstrate their laziness by refusing to walk and having to be carried on someone else's back. Others constantly yawn and lie down at every opportunity. In this way, many attempt to convince the princess of how lazy they are. Finally a young man shows up who simply approaches the princess and states that he has come to marry her as he is truly lazy. All the others, by attempting to show their laziness are not really lazy. The truly lazy man is lazy by nature and has no need or inclination for any demonstration. This is how it is when you know that you are *Brahman*. You simply are that. There's nothing you need to do about it and you don't necessarily feel any need to even speak about it, unless someone asks.

12.25 "To the jnani, it is absolutely evident that he is Brahman." Sri Siddharameshwar Maharaj

When you are in the waking state, you never need to say to yourself "I am alive." It is obvious to you. In just the same way, oneness with *Brahman* is evident to the realized person (*jnani*). This is because, for the realized person, the sense of "I," which was previously identified with the false center of the ego, has resolved itself back to its true center, which we call the Self. The ego has disappeared because its unreality was understood. It was maintained by the belief that it was real. Once that belief is released, the ego has no support and so it ceases to assert itself. Consciousness is now established in the Self, which is the true center, around which everything revolves and without which nothing can appear.

12.26 "Keep your faith in the unseen, that which is beyond the realm of reason." (Sri Siddharameshwar Maharaj)

The rest of this quotation is "*Jnanis* understand this and go their own way." After realization occurs, life shifts to another level. The ordinary worldly existence continues as before, but something has been added. There is a new understanding, a new consciousness of oneself existing beyond the mind. This new understanding puts everything else into perspective. What is false is seen to be false and is no longer confused with what is true. No effort is required to see this. It is just seen, just understood. So realized persons go their own way, without worrying about the world. They know that the world will take care of itself.

12.27 "The sign of a saint is that he does not act according to what comes into his mind." (Sri Siddharameshwar Maharaj)

You can be sure that whatever thoughts come to the mind of a realized person, he or she is not bound by them in any way. In ignorance, thoughts are assumed to be "mine." If "I" feel angry, "I" have no hesitation to express that anger. "I" feel totally justified in doing so. This is not the case with a realized person. Thoughts are thoughts. They arise from the vast ocean of nothingness that is the causal body and they return to it. If a thought is meant to be expressed in a particular moment, it will be expressed. If it is not meant to be expressed, it will not be. There is no compulsion to act on a desire or to express the thoughts that arise, because there is no identification of the Self with the "I," which is the sense of doership.

12.28 "One who has understood the path of no-mind has no care. He is always immersed in his own Self." (Sri Siddharameshwar Maharaj)

Sometimes it is asked "Why seek realization? What is the value of it?" Some seekers want to be reassured that there is some pleasure, some bliss to be had from realization, something that would make all their efforts worthwhile. Such seekers are generally disappointed with the answers they receive, because, in fact, the realization of the Self does not involve any gain or the acquiring of anything new. It is really the loss of what is not true, the abandonment of ignorance. The experience of realization is more like relief than bliss. Blissful experiences that come suddenly tend to be so striking because they are in contrast to the ordinary, rather dull state of the seeking mind. On the other hand, the seeker who has been following the path for a long time and is closer to realization, is already free from many petty anxieties and so, when the final understanding arrives, it may not seem so striking. In fact, it may be a relatively small shift at that point.

However it comes, final understanding means the end of all care. Mind has become no-mind and so there is no longer any false center to which care and anxiety can stick. Consciousness has turned back to its true center, where it remains immersed in itself, contemplating its own existence.

12.29 "The one who is steady in his Self says "I am all pervading, complete, and immanent in every heart." (Sri Siddharameshwar Maharaj)

When people go down to the River Ganga and take the water back to their homes in brass pots, they do not regard that water as separate from the river that it came from. They use it for worship and, for them, it represents the Goddess Ganga just as the river itself does. This is the correct attitude to have towards consciousness also.

The individual consciousness that each person feels in his or her heart is just the same as the universal consciousness that pervades everywhere. There is no difference at all. "All-pervading" means that it is immanent in all forms. It consists of the totality of the individual consciousness, just as a forest is made up of the individual trees. In fact, the concept of "individual consciousness" is false. There is only the one, undivided consciousness. Ignorance, bondage, consists of the belief that the individual consciousness is really separate. Liberation is seeing through that false assumption.

12.30 "The realized one does not have any concepts or thoughts." (Sri Siddharameshwar Maharaj)

There is a story about a man who had two sons. Both the sons were sent by their father to seek wisdom in a distant city. After some time, they returned home and their father asked them what they had learned about Truth. The older brother recited to his father many scriptural passages about the nature of *Brahman*: how the world had appeared in it through the power of *Maya*, but without affecting its essential Oneness, how the whole universe was contained in *Brahman*, how each one is That but does not realize it, and so on and so forth. When his father asked the younger son what he had learned of the Truth, he just stood in silence, feeling that to try to express anything of the Absolute Truth in words is to reduce it to the level of relative truth. Then his father knew that this son had found wisdom and had truly understood.

Silence is the natural condition of the realized person. As long as the dream of life continues, silence exists as pure consciousness that is aware of itself. When the dream comes to an end, silence remains as the Absolute, without consciousness of anything. This last statement, although logical, is theoretical. Nothing can be said about the condition of the Absolute after this consciousness has gone. We only know consciousness that is here now. That is the nature of consciousness. It *is* knowledge. The whole experience of birth, life, and death, occurs in knowledge, in the mind. After realization, this is seen and understood clearly and so the hold of knowledge, and the world that appears in it, is released. Concepts, thoughts, an entire universe may arise and disappear again. The Self is not involved in it and so is not concerned.

12.31 "The true mark of a saint is not taking the world to be true." (Sri Siddharameshwar Maharaj)

There are two birds in a tree. One of them constantly flits from branch to branch, eating the fruits that grow among the leaves. The other sits quietly at the top of the tree and does not taste or eat any of the fruits. The realized person is like the bird at the top of the tree. As far as he or she is concerned, the world is not true. It is nothing but a long dream. He or she has no desire for the transitory pleasures of life and so does not touch them. In this way, by not-doing, rather than by doing, and by silence rather than by speech, the realized person shows how to live in this world.

Glossary of Terms Used by Sri Ranjit Maharaj

The glossary covers most of the terms that Maharaj used on a regular basis in his talks. A quotation follows the definition of the term to provide an example of the context in which he used that word or phrase.

absolute: the final reality that is prior to both knowledge and ignorance, and all duality. See also *final reality, He, Parabrahman.*
Context: *"Yourself is He, without self, Absolute reality."*

address: an analogy for the correct knowledge given by the Master. Once the correct knowledge has been received, the aspirant must go in and take possession of the house, which is the Self.
Context: *"You can get the address, Master gives it to you, but he cannot come there with you. You have to go there and enter yourself."*

aspirant: a spiritual seeker who is ignorant of his or her true nature and who practices or follows a particular path.
Context: *"Due to ignorance you say that I am a Master and you are an aspirant but in fact the reality is you!"*

awakening: See *realization.*

birth and death: concepts that arise in ignorance. See also *forget your Self.*
Context: *"Due to ignorance you say "I've got the birth and I will die." Body dies you don't die."*

body: the temporary covering of gross matter. One of a long series.
Context: *"Many bodies have come and gone for you. Why you should worry for this body?"*

bondage: the concept that "I" exist and am not free. Compare with *liberation*. See also *seeking*.
Context: *"Nobody puts you in bondage. You take it on yourself."*

Brahman: the all-pervading aspect of knowledge or consciousness. Reality considered in the relative sense. Compare with *Parabrahman*. See also *knowledge, power*.
Context: *"Brahman is knowledge."*

causal body: the realm of complete absence of thought from which thought arises and into which it disappears. The causal body is pure ignorance or forgetfulness. It is called the causal body because, without it, thoughts and objects could not appear, that is; there has to be "nothing" in order for there to be "something." Peaceful, due to the absence of disturbance. It is perceived as emptiness or void by the ego. See also *ignorance, zero*.
Context: *"In the causal body, any thought may come at any time."*

consciousness: a synonym for knowledge. Not used much by Maharaj. See *knowledge*.

creator: the power that allows the names and forms to be projected by the mind. See also *God, power*.
Context: *"From knowledge everything happens. Knowledge is the creator."*

die: to come to the end of ignorance through Self-knowledge. The destruction of the ego as a center of volition.
Context: *"To die means to forget everything. When you are living, die in that way."*

doer: the imaginary entity that the ego conjures up when it says "I did it!"
Context: *"Ignorance is in thinking you are the doer."*

doing: the false concept, maintained by the ego, that it is responsible for what happens.
Context: *"You simply must get rid of this notion of doing, which is imprinted in*

your mind."

doubt: the absence of certainty that prevails when Self-knowledge is not there.
Context: *"Doubts are ignorance."*

dream: the spontaneous arising, in ignorance, of images and concepts, which are then taken to be true.
Context: *"Life is nothing but a long dream."*

duality: the separation of "I" and "the rest of the world" that occurs when the body is taken to be the Self. This false sense of separation disappears when you know yourself to be the one reality. See also *knowledge.*
Context: *"Duality makes you."*

ego: the concept or assumption that "I" exist as a separate individual. The ego is the embodiment of ignorance. Ego actually has no existence. It is merely imagined. However, where there is a belief it exists, it does exist. The cause and the effect are the same.
Context: *"The ego is like the barren woman's son. It doesn't exist but still you say "I've done it."*

final reality: the unmanifest oneness that in itself is not aware of itself. It becomes aware of itself through knowledge. In the final reality, knowledge is in the unmanifest state and exists only as potential. See also *He, Parabrahman.*
Context: *"On one side, the whole world is there. On the other, final reality."*

final understanding: the understanding that "I" do not exist and that therefore there is no one to understand and nothing to be understood.
Context: *"The final understanding is that you don't exist and He is always there."*

forgetting the mind: a state in which there is only awareness of oneness. The ego and the world are not true. Forgetting the mind means remembering one's Self.

Context: *"There is only one way, forget this and you know Him. No words for it."*

forgetting your Self: the original cause of ignorance. Forgetting the Self means remembering the ego.
Context: *"The source of consciousness itself is the forgetting or ignorance of the final reality."*

God: the manifest, or creative aspect of reality that pervades and gives life to everything. See also *creator, power*.
Context: *"God and his creation are not true when knowledge goes off."*

gold: an analogy for the all-pervading nature of reality or pure knowledge. Just as there are no ornaments without gold (no forms without the underlying substance), gold (substance) does not manifest without form. Substance is pure knowledge/universal consciousness/Brahman, but that substance in itself is not a thing. It manifests through form. Therefore the whole creation is Brahman.
Context: *"All the ornaments are nothing but gold."*

grace: the power to accept the Master's teaching. The mind cannot control this power and so it appears to come from a higher level. Actually it is one's own power, one's own Self. The Self is seeking Itself through the seeker.
Context: *"What the Master says, accept it. That is the grace."*

He: the manifest aspect of reality, the pure knowledge or universal consciousness that is the substance in all forms. See also *power*.
Context: *"Understand the power. You are the power. You are He."*

I: the Self or final reality. However, "I" is appropriated by the ego to refer to the imaginary entity that it takes itself to be.
Context: *"You never forget yourself. You're always there. But you misrepresent the "I."*

ignorance: an imaginary state, characterized by a belief in what does not exist. See also *ego*.

Context: *"Ego is ignorance. By understanding you can overcome ignorance."*

illusion: See *ignorance.*
Context: *"Whatever can be experienced is illusion."*

kick: the identification with objects that makes them seem real and important.
Context: *"You say it's true because you are in the kick of ignorance."*

knowledge: the power, the consciousness that pervades everywhere. Knowledge is misinterpreted in the body and mind as the illusion of individual existence as a person, who then becomes an object. This false knowledge arises from ignorance and is the mula Maya, or original illusion. When this knowledge arises, in early childhood, and also every morning when the body and mind "wake up," the whole world appears. There is no knowledge in deep sleep or in the final reality. See also *Brahman, power, pure knowledge.*
Context: *"That knowledge is yourself, one should understand that. Then you become the creator of the world."*

liberation: the understanding that there never was any one to be bound. Compare with *bondage.*
Context: *"Bondage and liberation is also mind's work. Why do you want liberation? No need for it."*

mahakarana body: the realm of pure knowledge. A self-illuminating or self-evident presence. Self-knowledge. This state is realized when the aspirant understands that he or she is aware of the nothingness of the causal body. See also *pure knowledge.*

Master: a realized person who gives the true facts about illusion and reality. The Master who appears as another human being points to the fact that the true Master is the Self, and is not other than the aspirant.
Context: *"The Master is everywhere. He is never away from you, you and he are one."*

Maya: from Sanskrit "that which is not." See *ignorance.*

Context: *"Say it is not true, then an end comes to that knowledge, and that ends Maya."*

mind: the subtle level in which thoughts appear. Thoughts can be of the illusory "I" or they can be the correct thoughts given by the Master. See also *thought.*
Context: *"The mind is your greatest enemy and your greatest friend."*

name and form: the illusory aspects of the world, for example, the attributes of body and mind that are assumed at birth and dropped at death.
Context: *"Only the name and form which are illusion disappear."*

no-mind: the condition of stillness and openness that the mind comes to when it accepts the correct thoughts and is no longer dominated by ego.
Context: *"Reality is oneness, non-duality, no-mind."*

not true: a superimposition or appearance only, without existence apart from the underlying reality. Everything that happens is appearance only, like a reflection in a mirror. The reflection is not the reality, and so reality remains untouched by anything that appears. See also *gold.*
Context: *"The world you see is nothing but a reflection of reality. Reflection cannot be true."*

oneness: the condition of non-duality, in which there is no sense of separation between "I" and "the rest of the world." Compare with *duality.*
Context: *"There is only oneness, so whatever you see and perceive is He."*

Parabrahman: the final reality that is the attributeless aspect of Brahman or pure knowledge. Para means beyond, so Parabrahman indicates non-relative Brahman, or Brahman considered as the absolute. Compare with *Brahman.* See also *final reality, He.*
Context: *"Parabrahman is He, and He is everywhere."*

power: the all-pervading knowledge or universal consciousness that is the manifest aspect of reality. The sense of self-existence that animates a form, like electricity when it is connected to an appliance. See also *creator, God, He.*
Context: *"If you understand you're not the body, then you are the power that is in you. You are everywhere."*

pure knowledge: the abstract, all-pervading aspect of knowledge. The principle that inhabits all forms. Knowledge is experienced in its pure form in the mahakarana body, where it is free from any trace of ignorance. See also *He, power.*
Context: *"Pure knowledge is not ego. Pure knowledge is He."*

reality: See *final reality.*
Context: *"Reality is not a state. It is stateless."*

realization: the final understanding of one's true nature. A permanent change of being that includes the understanding that there is no "doer." Spiritual seeking ends with realization, because it is understood that one has always been what one was seeking. See also *Self knowledge.*
Context: *"If you want to be realized, you have to throw off the mind."*

realized person: one who has understood that he is reality and that nothing exists apart from Him. He may not appear different to anyone else, but inside he has complete conviction of his own nature and that of the world and is at peace, without need of anything.
Context: *"Try to understand the realized person, what they say. They say they have not done anything in their life."*

sat-chit-ananda: the being-knowledge-fullness which is playing in everything and enjoying itself through all the various forms. See also *He, pure knowledge, power.*
Context: *"Sat-chit-ananda is everywhere. It is the original seed."*

screen: the original condition of permanence and oneness, the unchanging background against which the show of the objective

world appears. See also *Self.*
Context: *"Reality is ever there, just like a screen. Pictures come and go, and the screen doesn't care."*

seeking: the condition that arises with the concept "I am bound and therefore must seek liberation." See also *bondage, liberation.*
Context: *"Kill the seeker! Nothing to be sought."*

Self: (with capital S): the eternal subject that is the true nature of all things. (Same word with small s signifies ego.) See also *final reality, Self-knowledge.*
Context: *"Body is not Self. Mind is not Self. Knowledge is not Self. Final reality is Self."*

Self knowledge: the absolute conviction that I am He, the reality. The knowledge of one's true nature. This knowledge means the end of seeking and the end of ignorance. See also *realization.*

Self realization: See *realization.*

sky: the causal body or ignorance from which knowledge arises. See also *causal body, zero.*
Context: *"The sky is zero. A big cyclone comes in the sky. It makes havoc, then it goes."*

source: the stateless state or no-mind condition that is prior to the appearance of knowledge or thought. See also *final reality.*
Context: *"When I go to the source of myself, I disappear."*

subtle body: the realm of the mind.

supra-causal body: See *mahakarana body.*

thought: a concept, image, or belief that arises. There is no separate thinker. The thought itself creates the thinker.
Context: *"Bad and good thoughts come and go on you. They don't remain. Thoughts are like the wind."*

touch: taking something in illusion to be true and identifying oneself with it.
Context: *"You take the touch of the body and you say I'm this."*

understanding: an inner transformation that occurs when the aspirant sees the truth of one of the Master's teachings. A combination of emotional force from the heart and logic from the intellect.
Context: *"With wrong understanding you become wrong. With right understanding you become right."*

universal consciousness: the impersonal, pure knowledge that inhabits all forms. See also *power, pure knowledge.*
Context: *"When you understand that you are not the body, your consiousness becomes universal."*

witnessing: a quality of knowledge in the mahakarana body that sees the objects that appear but does not identify itself with them or say "mine." In the final reality, witnessing is not true, because in oneness there is no seer and no seen.
Context: *"If you forget the witnessing, then you don't remain, otherwise you are still there. The one who witnesses always remains."*

zero: ignorance and what is perceived through ignorance. Whatever is not the one reality. Whatever does not exist. See also *forgetting your Self, ignorance, Maya.*
Context: *"You forget yourself and that means zero and then everything starts."*